Strings Of Brilliance: Mastering Melody and Harmony Development For Guitar Composition

University Scholastic Press

UNIVERSITY SCHOLASTIC PRESS
New York   London   Rome

Other Musician's Series Books
By University Scholastic Press:

A Guitarist's Grimoire: Unlocking the Secrets of Creating A Musical Diary To Master Guitar Composition

Storytelling With Sound: Fundamentals of Creative Guitar Composition

Musical Architecture Secrets: Structure Planning For Guitar Composition

Strings Of Brilliance: Mastering Melody and Harmony Development For Guitar Composition

Rhythm Mastery for Guitarists: Unlocking Tempo and Timing Techniques For Guitar Composition

Table Of Contents

INTRODUCTION

Welcome to a journey through the vibrant and dynamic world of guitar composition. In this comprehensive guide, we embark on an exhilarating exploration of melody and harmony development tailored specifically for the aspiring guitarist. Whether you're a seasoned player seeking to refine your craft or a newcomer eager to unlock the secrets of musical expression, this book is your definitive roadmap to melodic and harmonic brilliance.

Within the following pages, we will unravel the mysteries of melody and harmony, empowering you to unleash your full musical potential on the fretboard. Each chapter is meticulously crafted to provide you with the tools, techniques, and insights needed to captivate listeners with your compositions. From understanding the anatomy of the guitar to mastering advanced harmonization techniques, every aspect of melody and harmony development is explored with authority and precision.

In **Melody Development**, we lay the groundwork for crafting unforgettable musical journeys, delving into the nuances of repetition within phrases and dynamic variation to infuse your compositions with depth and emotion.

Musical Context invites you to consider the broader landscape in which your compositions exist, guiding you to create melodies and harmonies that resonate with your audience on a profound level.

Scale and Interval Choices empowers you to navigate the vast array of musical possibilities, enabling you to make informed decisions that enhance the expressiveness of your compositions.

As we journey through chapters such as **Smooth Phrasing** and **Call and Response**, you'll discover how to create melodies that flow effortlessly and engage listeners with captivating musical dialogue.

In the realm of harmony development, chapters like **Harmonization Techniques** and **Harmonic Layers** offer invaluable insights into crafting lush, rich harmonic landscapes that complement your melodies beautifully.

With guidance on **Feedback** and the importance of **Iteration**, you'll learn to refine your compositions with precision, continually pushing the boundaries of your musical prowess.

As you embark on this transformative journey, remember that creativity knows no bounds. Embrace both complexity and simplicity, and let your intuition be your guide as you explore the rich tapestry of melody and harmony on the guitar.

With dedication, perseverance, and the guidance found within these pages, you are poised to unlock a world of musical possibilities. So pick up your guitar, and let the melodies and harmonies within you soar to new heights of expression.

MELODY DEVELOPMENT

Develop your initial melodic ideas into cohesive phrases.

COHESIVE PHRASING

Developing your initial melodic ideas into cohesive phrases is a crucial step in the process of creating a compelling guitar composition. This involves expanding and refining your initial musical thoughts into well-formed and expressive melodies.

Let's explore how this development best evolves.

MELODIC SEED

Begin with a strong melodic seed, which could be a short musical idea or motif. This seed will serve as the foundation for the development of your melody.

Developing a strong melodic seed is a fundamental and impactful step in the creation of a compelling guitar composition. This initial melodic idea serves as the foundation upon which the entire musical piece is built.

Establishing a Musical Identity:

Why: A strong melodic seed provides the composition with a unique and identifiable musical identity.

How: Craft a short, distinctive motif that captures the essence and emotional tone of your composition.

Conveying Emotion and Theme:

Why: Melodies are powerful conveyors of emotion. A well-developed seed sets the emotional tone and can convey themes or narratives.

How: Choose a key and mode that align with the intended emotional and thematic content of your composition.

Creating Memorable Hooks:

Why: A strong melodic seed often contains memorable and catchy elements, creating a musical hook that resonates with listeners.

How: Focus on simplicity, incorporating intervals or rhythmic patterns that leave a lasting impression.

Providing Direction for Composition:

Why: The melodic seed acts as a guiding force, providing direction for the overall composition.

How: Use the melodic seed as a reference point to structure subsequent sections, creating a cohesive and well-connected piece.

Establishing Harmonic Foundations:

Why: The melodic seed influences harmonic choices, laying the groundwork for chord progressions and harmonies throughout the composition.

How: Identify chord tones within the melodic seed, ensuring alignment with the underlying harmonies.

Encouraging Cohesion and Unity:

Why: A strong melodic seed promotes cohesion, tying together different sections of the composition.

How: Strategically repeat and vary the melodic seed, maintaining a sense of unity while allowing for creative exploration.

Enhancing Playability on Guitar:

Why: Considering the playability of the melodic seed ensures that your composition is accessible to guitarists.

How: Experiment with guitar-friendly techniques, voicings, and positions to make the melodic seed both expressive and playable.

Allowing for Creative Exploration:

Why: The melodic seed serves as a launchpad for creative exploration, inspiring new ideas and variations.

How: Improvise around the melodic seed, allowing for spontaneous ideas to emerge and contribute to the composition's development.

Capturing Listener Attention:

Why: A compelling melodic seed captures the listener's attention from the start, drawing them into the musical journey.

How: Focus on creating an opening statement that is engaging and intriguing, inviting the listener to delve deeper into the composition.

Fostering Emotional Resonance:

Why: Emotional resonance is a key aspect of memorable compositions. A strong melodic seed establishes an emotional connection with the audience.

How: Experiment with dynamics, articulation, and phrasing within the melodic seed to evoke specific emotions.

Building a Foundation for Improvisation:

Why: If your composition involves improvisation, a strong melodic seed provides a solid foundation for improvisational exploration.

How: Allow the melodic seed to guide improvisational moments, providing a thematic anchor within the spontaneous elements.

Supporting Harmonic and Melodic Development:

Why: The melodic seed is a catalyst for harmonic and melodic development, driving the composition forward.

How: Introduce variations, extensions, and dynamic changes to evolve the melodic seed as the composition progresses.

Setting the Tone for Sections:

Why: Each section of your composition can be introduced or characterized by elements derived from the melodic seed.

How: Use the melodic seed to establish motifs that recur in various sections, creating a sense of continuity.

Providing a Framework for Collaboration:

Why: If collaborating with others, a clear and strong melodic seed offers a shared framework for creative contributions.

How: Share the melodic seed with collaborators, allowing them to build upon and contribute to the composition cohesively.

In summary, developing a strong melodic seed is a foundational step that influences the entire composition. It sets the tone, provides direction, and becomes a musical identity that listeners can connect with. Through careful crafting, iteration, and exploration, your melodic seed can evolve into a captivating and memorable musical journey on the guitar.

MUSICAL CONTEXT

Consider the musical context of your composition. Understand the key, mode, and harmonic progression, as these elements will influence the development of your melody.

UNDERSTANDING MUSICAL CONTEXT

Embarking on the intricate journey of crafting a guitar composition is akin to navigating a rich musical landscape, where every note resonates with purpose and emotion.

As you delve into the realms of melody, understanding the musical context is your compass, guiding you through the labyrinth of possibilities and aiding in the development of a truly captivating piece.

Picture this: you're seated with your guitar, strings humming under your fingertips, ready to breathe life into a melody that exists only in the recesses of your imagination. To truly elevate your composition, it is paramount to consider the broader musical context in which it will thrive.

Here is a roadmap to navigating musical context.

Harmonic Awareness:

Harmony is the bedrock upon which your melody dances. Familiarize yourself with the harmonic structure of your composition. What chords are you working with? How do they interact and progress? Understanding the harmonic context empowers you to craft a melody that not only complements but enhances the underlying harmony.

Rhythmic Dynamics:

The rhythmic heartbeat of your composition sets the pulse for your melody. Is it a lively, upbeat piece or a contemplative ballad? Align the rhythmic nuances of your melody with the tempo and feel of your composition. This synchronization creates a seamless flow, captivating your audience and immersing them in the musical journey.

Emotional Palette:

Every melody is a vessel for emotion. Consider the emotional landscape you wish to paint with your composition. Is it a jubilant celebration or a melancholic introspection? Infuse your melody with the emotive colors that resonate with the overarching sentiment, allowing your audience to connect on a profound level.

Stylistic Identity:

Whether you're channeling the soulful blues, the intricate fingerstyle of classical guitar, or the raw energy of rock, understanding the stylistic context is pivotal. Each genre carries its own set of rules and traditions. Embrace and embellish these stylistic elements to craft a melody that not only fits but stands out within its musical milieu.

Dynamic Storytelling:

Think of your melody as a narrative, weaving through the musical landscape, telling a story without words. Consider the highs and lows, the tension and release. Create dynamic arcs within your melody, allowing it to unfold organically and captivate your audience with its storytelling prowess.

Empathetic Crafting:

As you navigate this intricate process, empathize with your composition. Feel its heartbeat, understand its aspirations. Allow your musical intuition to guide your fingers across the frets, forging a connection between your artistic intent and the evolving melody.

In the grand tapestry of music, the melody is your signature, your voice in a vast symphony. By comprehending the musical context, you empower your melody to not merely exist but to flourish and resonate deeply with those who experience it. So, embark on this journey with confidence, and let the musical context be your steadfast companion, guiding you toward the zenith of melodic brilliance.

SCALE AND INTERVAL CHOICES

Experimenting with different scales and intervals is a fantastic way to expand your melodic vocabulary in guitar composition. This exploration opens up new sonic possibilities, allowing you to create fresh, unique, and captivating melodies.

EXPERIMENTING WITH SCALES AND INTERVALS

Any melodic development is dependent on your scale and interval choices. Let's dive deep to inspire your melodic development.

Familiarize Yourself with Various Scales:
Explore a variety of scales beyond the standard major and minor scales. Consider modes (e.g., Dorian, Mixolydian, Phrygian), pentatonic scales, blues scales, exotic scales (e.g., harmonic minor, melodic minor), and modal interchange. Each scale brings its own character and flavor to your melodic vocabulary.

Mix and Match Scales:
Experiment with combining different scales within a single composition. For instance, you might start a phrase in a major scale and transition seamlessly into a harmonic minor scale. This mixing of scales adds complexity and interest to your melodic development.

Explore Uncommon Intervals:
Move beyond the typical whole and half steps. Experiment with uncommon intervals, such as augmented and diminished intervals. Incorporate wide

intervals, like sixths and sevenths, to create expansive and intervallic melodic lines.

Use Chromaticism:

Integrate chromatic passages into your melodies. Chromaticism involves using notes outside the diatonic scale, adding tension and unpredictability. When used judiciously, chromaticism can bring a modern and sophisticated touch to your compositions.

Experiment with Microtonality:

Delve into microtonal playing by exploring intervals smaller than a semitone. This unconventional approach can lead to unique and exotic melodic expressions. Slide between microtonal intervals for a fluid and expressive sound.

Examples of Experimentation with Scales and Intervals:

Mixing Major and Dorian Modes:
Original Motif (Major): C - D - E
Variation (Dorian): C - D - E♭
Experiment by starting with a major scale motif and shifting to the Dorian mode for a subtle but effective change in mood.

Combining Pentatonic and Blues Scales:
Original Motif (Pentatonic): A - C - D
Variation (Blues): A - C - D - D♯
Mix the pentatonic scale with the blues scale to introduce a bluesy flavor to your melodic development.

Exploring Diminished Intervals:

Original Motif: E - G - B

Variation (Diminished): E - G♭ - A♯

Experiment with diminished intervals to add tension and a sense of unpredictability to your melodic ideas.

Utilizing Wide Intervals:

Original Motif: G - B

Variation (Sixths): G - E

Incorporate wide intervals, like sixths, to create a more expansive and open sound in your melodies.

Chromatic Passages for Tension:

Original Motif: F - A - C

Variation (Chromatic): F - F♯ - G - A

Add a touch of chromaticism within your melody to introduce tension and intrigue.

Microtonal Slides:

Original Motif: D - E - F

Variation (Microtonal): D - E - F (microtonal slide to F♯)

Experiment with microtonal slides for a subtle yet distinctive shift in pitch within your melodic phrases.

Modal Interchange:

Original Motif: A - Bm - D

Variation (Mixolydian Interchange): A - Bm - D7

Explore modal interchange by introducing a dominant seventh chord within a progression, altering the harmonic context and influencing the melodic development.

Experimenting with different scales and intervals is a limitless playground for your melodic creativity on the guitar. By pushing the boundaries of traditional scales and exploring unconventional intervals, you breathe life into your compositions, making them more vibrant and distinctive. Use these examples as a starting point, but don't be afraid to venture into uncharted territory. The beauty of experimentation lies in the discovery of unique sounds that resonate with your personal style and artistic vision.

REPETITION WITHIN PHRASES

Use repetition strategically within your phrases. Repeating certain melodic motifs or sequences establishes familiarity and strengthens the overall structure of the melody.

STRATEGIC USE OF REPETITION

Strategic use of repetition within phrases is a powerful tool for melodic development in guitar composition. Repetition not only enhances memorability but also establishes motifs, reinforces thematic elements, and contributes to the overall cohesion of your composition.

Let's explore how to employ repetition strategically, along with examples to illustrate its effectiveness:

Establish a Core Motif:

Start by creating a core motif – a short melodic idea that encapsulates the essence of your composition. This motif serves as the foundation upon which you can build and develop your melody. Repetition of this motif provides a sense of continuity and familiarity.

Varying Repetition:

Experiment with variations of the core motif through repetition. This could involve altering the rhythm, adding embellishments, or transposing the motif to a different octave. Varying the repetition prevents monotony while maintaining a thematic connection.

Creating Musical Hooks:

Repetition is instrumental in crafting memorable musical hooks. Identify key phrases or motifs within your composition that possess inherent catchiness, and strategically repeat them. These hooks serve as anchor points for the listener, leaving a lasting impression.

Examples of Strategic Repetition:

Repeating a Core Motif:

Original Motif: E - D - C

Repetition 1: E - D - C

Repetition 2: E - D - C

By repeating the core motif, you establish a recognizable melodic element that becomes a central theme in your composition.

Varying Repetition with Embellishments:

Original Motif: G - A - B

Repetition 1 (Embellished): G - A - B - A - G

Repetition 2 (Transposed): D - E - F - E - D

Vary the repetition by embellishing the motif with additional notes or transposing it to create nuanced variations.

Creating Hooks with Catchy Phrases:

Original Motif: A - C - D

Repetition 1: A - C - D

Repetition 2 (Hook): A - C - D - D - C

Identify a catchy phrase within your melody and repeat it strategically to create a memorable hook.

Sequential Repetition:

Original Motif: B - G - D

Repetition 1: B - G - D

Repetition 2 (Sequential): B - G - D - E - B - G - D

Use sequential repetition to extend and develop your motif gradually, creating a sense of progression.

Layering Repetition with Harmonies:

Original Motif: F - E - D

Repetition 1: F - E - D

Repetition 2 (Harmonized): F - E - D (harmonized in thirds)

Experiment with harmonizing the repeated motif to add depth and richness to your melodic development.

Dynamic Repetition in Crescendo:

Original Motif: G - F - E

Repetition 1: G - F - E

Repetition 2 (Crescendo): G - F - E (gradually increasing dynamic intensity)

Apply dynamic repetition by gradually increasing the volume or intensity of the repeated motif.

Integrating Repetition in a Call-and-Response:

Original Motif: D - A - B

Repetition 1 (Call): D - A - B

Repetition 2 (Response): D - A - B - B - A

Use repetition in a call-and-response structure to create a dialog between melodic phrases.

Strategic repetition within phrases is a versatile and effective technique for enhancing melodic development in guitar composition. By carefully repeating and varying motifs, you establish thematic coherence, engage the listener's ear, and craft memorable musical moments. Experiment with different approaches to repetition, and let it become a dynamic force that shapes the identity and impact of your guitar compositions.

DYNAMIC VARIATION

Use dynamic variation to enhance the expressiveness of your melody. Gradual swells and fades, as well as changes in playing intensity, contribute to the emotional impact of the phrase.

INCORPORATING DYNAMICS

Using dynamic variation is a crucial element for enhancing the expressiveness of melodic development in guitar composition. Dynamics, the variations in volume and intensity, play a significant role in shaping the emotional impact of your music. By skillfully manipulating dynamics, you can add depth, nuance, and a compelling sense of narrative to your melodies.

Let's explore how to use dynamic variation effectively, along with examples to illustrate its impact on melodic development:

Gradual Swells and Fades:

Experiment with gradual increases and decreases in volume to create swells and fades within your melodic phrases. This technique can be particularly effective in building tension and releasing it in a controlled manner.

Example:

Original Phrase: A - B - C

Swell: Start softly on A, gradually increase volume through B, and peak on C.

Accentuating Important Notes:

Identify key notes within your melody and accentuate them with a slightly increased volume. This draws attention to crucial moments, emphasizing the emotional core of your composition.

Example:

Original Phrase: G – A – B

Accentuated Note: Play A with a slightly higher volume to highlight its significance.

Using Crescendos and Decrescendos:

Employ crescendos (gradual increase in volume) and decrescendos (gradual decrease in volume) to create dynamic arcs within your melodic phrases. This adds a sense of movement and drama to your composition.

Example:

Original Phrase: D – E – F

Crescendo: Gradually increase volume from D to F.

Employing Dynamic Contrasts:

Introduce dynamic contrasts by alternating between loud and soft passages. This creates a dynamic range that captivates the listener's attention and enhances the overall expressiveness.

Example:

Loud Passage: Play a segment of the melody with increased volume.

Soft Passage: Follow with a quieter segment for contrast.

Dynamic Picking and Strumming:

Experiment with dynamic variations in your picking or strumming technique. Varying the attack and intensity of your playing hand can add a rhythmic and dynamic dimension to your melodic development.

Example:

Original Picking: Gently pluck the strings for a soft passage.

Dynamic Picking: Introduce a more aggressive picking style for a louder and intense section.

Emotional Climaxes with Dynamics:

Use dynamics to build towards emotional climaxes within your composition. Gradually increase the volume and intensity as you approach these climactic points, creating a powerful and impactful musical moment.

Example:

Climactic Point: A powerful chord or high note.

Build-up: Gradually increase volume and intensity in the lead-up to the climactic point.

Dynamics in Call-and-Response Patterns:

Apply dynamic variations in call-and-response patterns to emphasize the interplay between phrases. This technique enhances the conversational quality of your melodic development.

Example:

Call: Play the initial phrase softly.

Response: Answer with a louder and more dynamically intense phrase.

Dynamic Articulations in Soloing:

When soloing, experiment with dynamic articulations such as bends, slides, and vibrato. Varying the intensity of these techniques adds expressive nuances to your melodic lines.

Example:

Vibrato: Introduce a wide and expressive vibrato during a sustained note for added emotional depth.

Silence as a Dynamic Element:

Utilize moments of silence as a dynamic element. A sudden pause can create a powerful contrast and add tension to your melodic development.

Example:

Original Phrase: C – D – E

Dynamic Pause: Briefly pause after D before resolving to E.

Dynamic Variation in Chord Progressions:

Apply dynamic variations in chord progressions by playing certain chords louder or softer. This technique shapes the harmonic landscape and influences the overall mood of your composition.

Example:

Louder Chords: Emphasize certain chords within a progression to create dynamic peaks.

Dynamic variation is a nuanced and expressive tool that can elevate the emotional impact of your melodic development on the guitar. By mastering the art of dynamics, you add layers of complexity, drama, and subtlety to your compositions. Experiment with these techniques, and let dynamic variation become an integral part of your toolkit for creating compelling and emotionally resonant guitar melodies.

ARTICULATION AND MELODIC PHRASES

Experiment with articulation techniques such as legato, staccato, slides, and hammer-ons/pull-offs. These techniques can add nuance and character to your melodic phrases.

EMPLOYING ARTICULATION TECHNIQUES

Articulation techniques play a pivotal role in shaping the nuance and character of melodic phrases in guitar composition. Mastering various articulation techniques allows you to infuse your playing with expressiveness, dynamics, and a distinctive voice.

Below are different articulation techniques to consider as you develop your melody.

Hammer-Ons and Pull-Offs:

Hammer-Ons (HO): Striking a note, then using a subsequent finger to tap a higher fret without picking again.

Pull-Offs (PO): Plucking a note, then using a subsequent finger to pull off to a lower fret without picking again.

Experimentation Tip:

Combine hammer-ons and pull-offs within a melodic phrase to create smooth and legato lines.

Slides:

Slide Up (SLU): Moving from a lower fret to a higher one by sliding the finger along the string.

Slide Down (SLD): Moving from a higher fret to a lower one by sliding the finger along the string.

Experimentation Tip:

Experiment with different slide lengths to evoke varying degrees of tension and emotion within your melodic phrases.

Bends:

Bend (B): Gradually raising the pitch of a note by pushing the string across the fretboard.

Release Bend (RB): Returning a bent note to its original pitch.

Experimentation Tip:

Vary the speed and intensity of your bends to explore different expressive qualities. Experiment with bending multiple strings simultaneously for a harmonically rich effect.

Vibrato:

Vibrato (V): Rapidly fluctuating the pitch of a sustained note to add warmth and expressiveness.

Experimentation Tip:

Adjust the speed and width of your vibrato to match the emotional context of your melodic phrases. Experiment with using vibrato on different strings and frets.

Tremolo Picking:

Tremolo Picking (TP): Rapidly picking a single note or a series of notes in quick succession.

Experimentation Tip:

Use tremolo picking to add intensity to specific moments within your melodic development.

Experiment with varying the speed of your tremolo picking for different effects.

Tapping:

Tapping (T): Using the fingers of the picking hand to tap the fretboard and produce notes without using the picking hand.

Experimentation Tip:

Incorporate tapping into your melodic phrases for rapid and dynamic bursts of sound. Experiment with combining tapping and conventional fretting techniques for intricate and unique melodic expressions.

Palm Muting:

Palm Muting (PM): Resting the palm of your picking hand lightly on the strings near the bridge to dampen their vibrations.

Experimentation Tip:

Introduce palm muting selectively within your melodic phrases to create a percussive and controlled sound. Experiment with varying the degree of palm muting for different tonal textures.

Staccato and Legato:

Staccato (ST): Playing notes in a short and detached manner.

Legato (LG): Playing notes in a smooth and connected manner.

Experimentation Tip:

Combine staccato and legato articulations to create contrast within your melodic phrases. Experiment with staccato for rhythmic emphasis and legato for fluidity.

Artificial Harmonics:

Artificial Harmonic (AH): Producing harmonics by lightly touching the string with the index finger while picking with the thumb.

Experimentation Tip:

Integrate artificial harmonics strategically within your melodic phrases to add ethereal and bell-like tones. Experiment with different frets and string positions for varied harmonic effects.

Fingerstyle Techniques:

Fingerstyle (FS): Plucking the strings with the fingers instead of a pick.

Thumb Slap (TS): Striking the strings with the thumb to produce a percussive sound.

Experimentation Tip:

Embrace fingerstyle techniques to add a diverse range of tones to your melodic phrases. Experiment with combining fingerstyle playing with conventional picking for a hybrid approach.

Experimenting with articulation techniques is a key aspect of developing a unique and expressive voice on the guitar. As you explore these techniques, remember that subtlety and control are essential. Use articulations not just as technical embellishments but as tools to convey emotion and enhance the storytelling aspect of your melodic composition. Tailor your articulation choices to the mood and narrative of your piece, and let your creativity flourish as you infuse your melodic phrases with depth and character.

ANATOMY OF THE GUITAR

Take advantage of the guitar's unique qualities, such as bends, vibrato, and string slides. These techniques can infuse your melody with a distinctive and expressive quality.

THE GUITAR'S UNIQUE QUALITIES

Delving into the expressive capabilities of the guitar, we uncover a rich tapestry of techniques that render it a truly unique instrument. Bends, vibrato, and string slides are not just embellishments; they are tools of melodic craftsmanship, allowing the guitarist to articulate emotions, shape tonality, and infuse their compositions with individuality.

Bending Realities:

Bending, a technique of altering pitch by physically manipulating the strings, is a hallmark of guitar expressiveness. Consider the iconic solo in Pink Floyd's *Comfortably Numb.* David Gilmour's bends epitomize controlled emotion, as he bends notes with precision, introducing a poignant narrative. Experiment with bending techniques, such as whole, half, and double bends, to articulate feelings ranging from yearning to triumph within your melody.

Vibrato's Subtle Embrace:

Vibrato, a controlled oscillation of pitch, is a nuanced technique that adds depth and warmth to each note. Eric Clapton's rendition of *Layla* showcases tasteful vibrato, enhancing the emotional resonance of the melody. Develop a sensitive touch; let vibrato be a tool for infusing character and soul into sustained notes, allowing your composition to breathe with a natural ebb and flow.

Sliding Through Dimensions:

String slides, whether subtle or pronounced, impart a sense of movement and continuity to your melody. Think of the opening riff in Led Zeppelin's *Whole Lotta Love*. Jimmy Page's slides create an arresting entrance, transforming static notes into a dynamic journey. Experiment with slides, exploring both ascending and descending movements, to add a compelling narrative arc to your melodic passages.

Harmonic Resonance:

Harmonics, achieved by lightly touching the strings at specific nodal points, produce ethereal, bell-like tones. Steve Vai's *Tender Surrender* showcases harmonic mastery, using artificial harmonics to create celestial textures. Integrate harmonics judiciously into your composition, allowing them to shimmer as celestial accents within the melodic landscape.

Tapping into Possibilities:

Finger tapping, popularized by Eddie Van Halen, expands the guitarist's toolkit. In *Eruption*, Van Halen employs tapping to create a whirlwind of cascading notes. While advanced, tapping can be subtly integrated into your composition for moments of heightened intensity or as a dynamic embellishment.

Fingerstyle Elegance:

Fingerstyle playing, whether through classical fingerpicking or contemporary techniques, unlocks a realm of possibilities. Consider Chet Atkins' rendition of *Mr. Sandman*, where intricate fingerstyle patterns elevate the melody. Embrace fingerstyle techniques to articulate individual notes, allowing for nuanced dynamics and rhythmic complexity.

In the hands of a skilled guitarist, these techniques transcend mere ornamentation. They become the means through which the instrument speaks, conveying the subtleties and nuances of the composer's vision. As you explore bends, vibrato, string slides, and beyond, view them not as isolated maneuvers but as interconnected elements within the guitarist's palette, contributing to the intricate canvas of your melodic expression. Mastery of these techniques transforms the guitar into a vessel of unparalleled emotive storytelling.

REGISTERS

Play around with different registers on the guitar. Moving between high and low registers can create a sense of movement and provide variety within your phrases.

EXPLORING DIFFERENT REGISTERS

Navigating the vast expanse of the guitar's registers is akin to exploring different sonic landscapes, each offering unique textures and possibilities for melodic development. From the deep resonance of low registers to the crystalline clarity of high registers, understanding and strategically employing these ranges is integral to crafting a captivating composition.

Low Register Groundwork:

The **low register**, encompassing the lower pitches of the guitar, provides a foundation of warmth and resonance. Think of the iconic opening riff in *Black Sabbath* by Black Sabbath. Tony Iommi's use of the low register creates a brooding, heavy atmosphere. Experiment with power chords, bass-heavy lines, and melodic motifs in the low register to establish a solid foundation for your composition.

Midrange Melodic Core:

The **midrange** is the heart of melodic expression, offering a balance between warmth and articulation. Consider the intricate fingerstyle of *Classical Gas* by Mason Williams. The midrange is where the intricate details of the melody come to life. Utilize this space for melodic intricacies, chord progressions, and the main thematic material of your composition.

High Register Brilliance:

The **high register**, comprising the upper pitches of the guitar, introduces brightness and clarity to your composition. The opening arpeggio in *Hotel California* by Eagles exemplifies the brilliance of the high register. Incorporate arpeggios, intricate picking patterns, and soaring lead lines in the high register to add brilliance and definition to your melody.

Transcending Octaves:

Exploring different octaves allows you to expand the sonic palette of your composition. In *Little Wing* by Jimi Hendrix, the melody moves seamlessly between different octaves, creating a sense of movement and exploration. Experiment with octave jumps, harmonies, and melodic motifs that traverse various registers, adding depth and interest to your guitar composition.

Dynamic Register Shifts:

Dynamic shifts between registers can be a powerful tool for melodic development. Take Metallica's *One*, for instance. The shift from a clean, melodic intro in the higher register to the heavy, distorted sections in the lower register creates a stark contrast. Use register shifts strategically to evoke different moods and intensities within your composition.

Embracing the Entire Fretboard:

A well-crafted melody should traverse the entire fretboard, utilizing the guitar's full range. Listen to *Sultans of Swing* by Dire Straits. Mark Knopfler seamlessly moves across registers, from intricate fingerpicking in the midrange to soaring lead lines in the high register. Embrace the versatility of the entire fretboard to create a melodic journey that unfolds across different tonal landscapes.

Incorporating various registers is not just about covering a range of pitches; it's about utilizing each register's unique sonic characteristics to convey different emotions and facets of your composition. As you venture into these melodic territories, view the registers as your sonic palette – each stroke, chord, or note contributing to the rich tapestry of your guitar composition.

SMOOTH PHRASING

Pay attention to the transitions between phrases. Use common tones or leading notes to connect phrases smoothly, creating a cohesive flow within your melody.

CONNECTING PHRASES

Creating a seamless flow between phrases is a crucial aspect of melodic development in guitar composition. Think of it as crafting a musical conversation where each phrase responds and interacts with the previous one.

Let's dive into techniques to connect phrases smoothly and explore examples that illustrate these principles.

The Art of Legato:

Legato, the technique of playing notes smoothly and connected, is a key player in achieving seamless transitions between phrases. Listen to Joe Satriani's *Always with Me, Always with You.* His use of legato allows each note to effortlessly glide into the next, creating a fluid and connected melodic journey. Experiment with hammer-ons, pull-offs, and slides to achieve legato passages that weave together like a musical tapestry.

Graceful Slides:

Introduce slides between notes or chords to add a touch of elegance and continuity. The intro to *Sultans of Swing* by Dire Straits showcases Mark Knopfler's masterful use of slides. The transitions are smooth and graceful, giving the melody a sense of fluidity. Incorporate slides judiciously to connect phrases and evoke a sense of movement within your composition.

Overlapping Phrasing:

Allow phrases to overlap, creating a seamless transition from one idea to the next. John Mayer's *Gravity* is a prime example. Notice how he lets certain notes linger while introducing the next phrase, creating a natural and overlapping progression. Experiment with sustained notes or chords that serve as a bridge, smoothly guiding the listener from one musical thought to the next.

Call and Response Dynamics:

Implement call and response dynamics between phrases. Think of the iconic riff in Led Zeppelin's *Whole Lotta Love*. The initial phrase serves as a call, and the response seamlessly connects to it. Utilize this conversational approach, letting each phrase answer or complement the previous one, creating a melodic dialogue.

Common Tones and Voice Leading:

Maintain a connection through common tones and thoughtful voice leading. In *Hotel California* by Eagles, notice how the solo incorporates shared notes, creating a sense of cohesion between phrases. Explore the fretboard to find common tones or smoothly guide the listener through a logical progression of notes, enhancing the connectivity of your melody.

Melodic Contour:

Pay attention to the overall melodic contour and shape of your phrases. In Eric Clapton's *Tears in Heaven*, the melody unfolds with a natural contour, creating a sense of continuity. Craft phrases that flow organically, allowing the melodic shape to guide the listener through a cohesive musical narrative.

Dynamic Expression:

Use dynamic expression to connect phrases by varying the intensity and emotion. Santana's *Europa* is a testament to expressive dynamics. The transitions between phrases are marked by shifts in intensity, creating a dynamic journey. Experiment with dynamics to infuse your melody with emotional nuances that serve as bridges between phrases.

As you explore these techniques, remember that smooth connectivity is not just about the technical execution but also about conveying a sense of emotion and purpose in your melodic storytelling. By mastering the art of seamless connection, your guitar composition becomes a journey that captivates the listener from phrase to phrase, leaving a lasting impression.

CALL AND RESPONSE AND MELODY

Develop call-and-response patterns within your melody. Play a phrase (call) and respond to it with a contrasting or complementary phrase. This adds conversational dynamics to your composition.

CREATING CALL AND RESPONSE PATTERNS

Crafting call-and-response patterns within your guitar composition is akin to having a musical conversation, where each phrase speaks and responds to the other. This dynamic interplay adds depth, interest, and a sense of narrative to your melody. Let's explore *how* to develop call-and-response patterns with precision and creativity.

Establish a Strong Call:

Begin with a compelling and distinctive call—a musical statement that draws attention. This can be a catchy riff, a memorable sequence of notes, or a rhythmic motif. Consider the iconic opening riff in *Sunshine of Your Love* by Cream. Clapton's guitar introduces a powerful call that becomes the focal point of the melody.

Craft a Thoughtful Response:

The response is equally crucial and should complement or answer the initial call. It can mirror the rhythm, echo a melodic fragment, or introduce a contrasting idea. In the context of *Sunshine of Your Love*, the response follows Clapton's call with a melodic phrase that complements the initial statement. Pay attention to the emotional and thematic nuances in your response to create a meaningful musical dialogue.

Explore Dynamics and Expression:

Vary dynamics and expression between the call and response to add nuance and interest. Think of Stevie Ray Vaughan's *Pride and Joy.* The opening call is assertive and dynamic, while the subsequent response introduces a more subdued, melodic contrast. Experiment with changes in volume, articulation, and intensity to enhance the dialogue between your phrases.

Use Rhythmic Contrast:

Introduce rhythmic contrast to distinguish between the call and response. If your call is rhythmically energetic, consider responding with a more relaxed or syncopated rhythm. In *Sweet Child o' Mine* by Guns N' Roses, the iconic guitar riff serves as a rhythmic call, while the subsequent response introduces a more flowing, melodic feel.

Spatial Awareness:

Allow for spatial awareness between the call and response. Give each phrase its moment to breathe before transitioning to the next. In the context of *Purple Haze* by Jimi Hendrix, the call–and–response patterns are punctuated by short breaks, creating a sense of anticipation and separation between the phrases.

Play with Intervallic Relationships:

Experiment with intervallic relationships between the call and response to add melodic interest. The opening of *Day Tripper* by The Beatles exemplifies this, with the call featuring a distinctive descending interval, followed by a response that ascends, creating a melodic conversation through intervallic variation.

Develop a Conversational Flow:

Think of your call-and-response patterns as a musical conversation. As one phrase speaks, the other responds in a way that complements, contrasts, or elaborates. This conversational flow can be found in *Blackbird* by The Beatles, where each guitar phrase responds to the previous one, creating a captivating and intimate musical dialogue.

By carefully developing call-and-response patterns within your melody, you transform your guitar composition into a dynamic and engaging narrative. This interplay between musical phrases not only captures the listener's attention but also provides a structure that guides the emotional journey of your composition. Embrace the art of musical conversation and let your guitar tell a story that resonates with depth and creativity.

ORNAMENTATION

Integrate ornamentation techniques, such as trills, grace notes, and mordents, to embellish and ornament your melodic ideas.

EXPERIMENTING WITH ORNAMENTATION

Ornamentation techniques in guitar playing are akin to adding intricate details and embellishments to a musical tapestry, enriching the melodic fabric with expressive nuances. Mastering these techniques allows you to infuse your composition with flair, creating a captivating and dynamic musical experience.

Below we list various ornamentation techniques and how to integrate them for melodic development.

Hammer-Ons and Pull-Offs:

Hammer-ons and pull-offs are fundamental ornamentation techniques that can add fluidity and agility to your melodies. Consider the opening of *Eruption* by Van Halen, where Eddie Van Halen's rapid hammer-ons and pull-offs create a cascade of notes. Integrate these techniques to connect notes seamlessly and introduce a sense of legato expressiveness.

Trills:

Trills involve the rapid alternation between two adjacent notes, typically embellishing a sustained note. In *Classical Gas* by Mason Williams, trills are used to add a touch of classical virtuosity. Experiment with trills to inject moments of ornate brilliance into your melody, enhancing its overall texture.

Slides:

Slides, whether short and subtle or long and expressive, can introduce a sense of movement and grace to your melodic lines. The solo in *Stairway to Heaven* by Led Zeppelin features Jimmy Page's masterful use of slides, creating a seamless connection between phrases. Utilize slides to navigate between notes or chords, adding a sonic dimension to your composition.

Bends and Vibrato:

Bends and vibrato, when employed judiciously, can elevate your melodic expression. Listen to the solo in *Comfortably Numb* by Pink Floyd, where David Gilmour's expressive bends and vibrato contribute to the emotional depth of the melody. Integrate controlled bends and vibrato to infuse your composition with a sense of emotion and character.

Grace Notes:

Grace notes, or embellishments that occur quickly before a main note, can introduce subtle ornamentation. In *Blackbird* by The Beatles, the addition of grace notes enhances the delicate beauty of the melody. Experiment with grace notes to add a touch of ornamentation to specific notes within your composition.

Harmonics:

Artificial harmonics, produced by lightly touching the strings at specific points, introduce ethereal and bell-like tones. In *Little Wing* by Jimi Hendrix, harmonics contribute to the otherworldly atmosphere of the melody. Incorporate harmonics sparingly to create moments of sonic intrigue and color.

Tremolo Picking:

Tremolo picking involves rapid repetition of a single note or alternation between two notes. It can add intensity and energy to your melodic lines. Listen to the tremolo picking in the intro of *Asturias* by Isaac Albéniz, adapted for guitar by Andrés Segovia. Experiment with tremolo picking to introduce dynamic and rhythmic variations into your composition.

Tapping:

Finger tapping allows you to create rapid and intricate patterns by tapping the fretboard with your picking hand. In *Eruption* by Van Halen, tapping is a central technique that propels the melody into the realm of virtuosity. Integrate tapping to introduce moments of percussive brilliance and technical prowess.

To effectively integrate ornamentation techniques, consider the emotional context of your composition. Use ornamentation to highlight key moments, convey specific emotions, or add complexity to your melodic lines. These techniques, when applied with intention and musicality, transform your guitar composition into a rich and ornamented tapestry of sound.

MELODIC SEQUENCES

Incorporate melodic sequences to extend and develop your phrases. A sequence involves repeating a pattern at different pitch levels, creating a sense of continuity and progression.

HOW TO USE MELODIC SEQUENCING

Melodic sequences are a powerful tool in guitar composition, allowing you to extend and develop musical phrases by repeating and transposing a specific pattern or motif. Incorporating melodic sequences adds coherence, continuity, and interest to your composition.

UNDERSTANDING MELODIC SEQUENCES

A melodic sequence is a repeating pattern of musical intervals, pitches, or rhythms. It can be a short motif, a scale fragment, or any identifiable sequence of notes that is repeated and transposed to different pitch levels. Sequences can ascend, descend, or follow more complex patterns, creating a sense of structure and unity within a melody.

HOW TO INCORPORATE MELODIC SEQUENCES

Identify a Motif or Pattern:
Begin by identifying a short and distinctive motif or pattern within your melody. This could be a specific set of notes, a scale fragment, or a rhythmic sequence that stands out.

Repeat the Motif:

Repeat the chosen motif consecutively within your melody. Repetition adds emphasis and helps establish a recognizable musical theme. This initial repetition sets the foundation for the development of the sequence.

Transpose the Motif:

Once you've repeated the motif, transpose it to a different pitch level. This can involve moving the entire motif up or down the scale, creating a new melodic statement while maintaining the original pattern.

Explore Ascending and Descending Sequences:

Experiment with both ascending and descending sequences. Ascending sequences build tension and energy, while descending sequences can bring resolution and a sense of conclusion. Alternating between these two types of sequences adds dynamic variety to your composition.

Combine Sequences:

Combine different types of sequences within your melody. For instance, you can have an ascending sequence followed by a descending one. This juxtaposition creates a sense of movement and complexity, enhancing the overall melodic development.

Use Sequences in Various Registers:

Apply melodic sequences across different registers of the guitar. This not only adds variety but also allows you to explore the full sonic range of the instrument.

Moving between higher and lower registers can create interesting contrasts.

Experiment with Rhythmic Variations:

Introduce rhythmic variations to your melodic sequences. Alter the rhythm while maintaining the pitch pattern, or vice versa. Syncopations, staccato notes, or triplet variations can inject rhythmic interest into the repeated motifs.

Example:

Consider the intro of *Sweet Child o' Mine* by Guns N' Roses. The ascending melodic sequence in the guitar riff follows a distinct pattern of notes, repeating and transposing as it climbs up the fretboard. This sequence not only establishes a memorable motif but also serves as the foundation for the melodic development throughout the song.

Incorporating melodic sequences allows you to create cohesive and engaging guitar compositions. By repeating and transposing specific patterns, you build a strong melodic framework that listeners can connect with. Experiment with different motifs, transpositions, and rhythmic variations to find the sequences that best suit the mood and direction of your composition.

CHORD TONES AND PASSING NOTES

Pay attention to chord tones and passing notes. Emphasize chord tones on strong beats for stability, and use passing notes for melodic embellishment and tension.

INTEGRATING CHORD TONES AND PASSING NOTES

Understanding and incorporating chord tones and passing notes into your guitar composition is a key aspect of melodic development. Chord tones provide stability and emphasize the underlying harmony, while passing notes add color and connect chord tones, creating fluid and expressive melodic lines.

CHORD TONES

Chord tones are the pitches that make up a chord. In the context of a specific harmony, emphasizing chord tones in your melody creates a strong connection with the underlying chords. These tones include the root, third, fifth, and seventh of a chord. Harmonizing your melody with these chord tones enhances the overall sense of harmony and coherence.

Incorporation:
1. Identify the chords in your progression.
2. Emphasize chord tones on strong beats of the measure.
3. Create melodic phrases that land on chord tones, providing points of resolution.
4. Use arpeggios to highlight individual chord tones.

Example:

Consider the opening riff of *Hotel California* by Eagles. The arpeggiated picking pattern emphasizes chord tones of the Bm, F, A, E, and Gm chords, providing a clear melodic connection to the harmonic structure.

PASSING NOTES

Passing notes are non-chord tones that connect chord tones, adding melodic interest and smooth transitions between harmonies. While passing notes may not belong to the underlying chord, they contribute to the overall melodic flow by creating a sense of movement and tension.

Incorporation:

1. Identify chord changes and the distances between chord tones.
2. Introduce passing notes to fill the gaps between chord tones.
3. Use passing notes on weaker beats or as part of melodic embellishments.
4. Experiment with chromatic passing notes for added color.

Example:

In the intro of *Wonderful Tonight* by Eric Clapton, passing notes are used to connect chord tones, creating a graceful and flowing melody. The use of passing notes between the chords contributes to the smooth and elegant character of the composition.

COMBINING CHORD TONES AND PASSING NOTES

Start and End with Chord Tones:
Begin and conclude melodic phrases with chord tones to establish a sense of stability and resolution.

Use Passing Notes for Motion:
Introduce passing notes in the middle of phrases to create a sense of motion and connect chord tones.

Explore Different Passing Note Types:
Experiment with diatonic passing notes within the scale, as well as chromatic passing notes, to add variety and color to your melodic lines.

Syncopation and Rhythmic Variation:
Apply passing notes on syncopated beats or incorporate rhythmic variations to enhance the dynamic aspect of your melodic development.

Example:
In the solo of *Comfortably Numb* by Pink Floyd, David Gilmour combines chord tones and passing notes masterfully. The solo features expressive bends and sustained notes on chord tones, while passing notes connect these moments, contributing to the emotive and narrative quality of the solo.

Incorporating chord tones and passing notes into your guitar composition enhances the depth and expressiveness of your melodies. By striking a balance between stability and movement, you create a captivating musical narrative that resonates with listeners. Experiment with these concepts in various musical contexts to discover their potential for enriching your melodic development on the guitar.

58

a captivating musical narrative that resonates with listeners. Experiment with these concepts in various musical contexts to discover their potential for enriching your melodic development on the guitar.

PHRASE LENGTHS

Be mindful of the length of your phrases. Varying the lengths of your melodic ideas contributes to the overall dynamic structure of your composition.

VARYING PHRASE LENGTHS

Varying the lengths of your melodic ideas is a powerful technique that adds dynamism, tension, and interest to your guitar composition. This strategic manipulation of melodic lengths contributes to the overall dynamic structure, creating a musical journey that captivates the listener's attention.

Let's explore how to effectively vary the lengths of your melodic ideas and understand the impact on the composition.

Short and Sweet:

Begin with concise and impactful melodic ideas. Short phrases or motifs act as musical statements, providing clarity and establishing the foundation for your composition. These brief bursts of melody create a sense of anticipation and set the stage for what's to come.

Prolonged Expressiveness:

Contrast shorter melodic ideas with more extended and expressive phrases. Allow certain moments in your composition to breathe by elongating specific melodic lines. This introduces depth, emotion, and a contemplative quality, providing a balance to the shorter, more punctuated elements.

Call and Response Dynamics:

Incorporate call-and-response dynamics by varying the lengths of your call and response phrases. A short, energetic call can be followed by a more extended and contemplative response, creating a conversational flow within your melody.

Climactic Buildups:

Gradually lengthen your melodic ideas as you build towards climactic moments in your composition. This technique is particularly effective in creating tension and anticipation. As your melodic ideas grow in length, the listener senses that a musical climax is imminent.

Unexpected Pauses:

Introduce unexpected pauses or rests within your melodic ideas. Silence can be a powerful tool. A brief pause following a shorter melodic idea can create suspense, while a longer pause after an extended phrase can emphasize the impact of what has just been played.

Rhythmic Diversity:

Vary the rhythmic complexity within your melodic ideas. Combine shorter, rhythmically intricate passages with longer, more sustained phrases. This rhythmic diversity adds texture and engages the listener's ear, preventing monotony in your composition.

Motivic Development:

Extend and develop specific motifs or themes. Take a short melodic idea introduced earlier in the composition and expand upon it, creating a sense of unity and development. This technique ties different sections of your composition together, providing a cohesive and interconnected feel.

Example:

Listen to the iconic solo in *Comfortably Numb* by Pink Floyd. David Gilmour uses varying melodic lengths to great effect. Short, emotive phrases are followed by extended, lyrical lines, creating a dynamic and evolving solo that contributes significantly to the overall emotional impact of the song.

IMPACT ON DYNAMIC STRUCTURE

Engagement and Interest:

Varying melodic lengths sustains listener engagement by preventing predictability. It keeps the musical narrative fresh and interesting.

Emotional Ebb and Flow:

Shorter melodic ideas provide bursts of emotion, while longer phrases offer moments of reflection and depth. This emotional ebb and flow contribute to the overall expressiveness of your composition.

Building Tension and Release:

The strategic use of shorter and longer melodic ideas contributes to the building and releasing of tension within your composition. The listener experiences peaks and valleys in intensity, creating a dynamic musical journey.

Structural Integrity:

Varying melodic lengths contributes to the structural integrity of your composition. It prevents monotony, ensuring that each section offers something unique in terms of melodic development.

By thoughtfully manipulating the lengths of your melodic ideas, you shape the narrative arc of your guitar composition. This dynamic interplay of short and long phrases engages the listener emotionally and maintains a sense of intrigue throughout the musical journey. Embrace the versatility of melodic lengths as a tool for crafting compelling and dynamic guitar compositions.

CLIMAXES

Build your melodic phrases towards climaxes or points of emotional intensity. This creates a sense of tension and release, adding drama to your composition.

BUILDING TOWARDS CLIMAXES

Building melodic phrases towards climaxes or points of emotional intensity is a crucial skill in creating dynamic and engaging guitar compositions. This technique allows you to guide the listener through a musical journey, building tension and anticipation before delivering a powerful and emotive climax.

Establish a Strong Foundation:

Begin your melodic journey with a solid foundation. This could be a simple motif, a catchy riff, or a memorable chord progression. Lay the groundwork for your composition by introducing elements that set the stage for emotional development.

Gradual Dynamic Ascension:

Build intensity gradually. Start your melodic phrases with a subdued dynamic, allowing room for expansion. This could involve softer picking, fewer notes, or a restrained rhythmic approach. As the phrase progresses, gradually increase the intensity by incorporating more notes, employing dynamic picking, or introducing rhythmic complexity.

Strategic Note Selection:

Be mindful of your note selection. As you approach the climactic point, consider using higher pitches, wide intervals, or notes that evoke emotion. These strategic choices contribute to the intensification of the melody and create a sense of rising energy.

Increase Articulation and Expression:

Intensify your playing through increased articulation and expression. This could involve adding vibrato to sustained notes, using dynamic techniques like hammer-ons and pull-offs, or employing slides for added expressiveness. These nuances contribute to the emotional depth of the melodic phrases.

Rhythmic Intensity:

Manipulate the rhythmic aspects of your phrases to build towards the climax. Introduce syncopation, double-time feel, or rhythmic variations as you approach the emotional peak. The rhythmic intensity enhances the forward momentum and heightens the sense of anticipation.

Expansive Fretboard Movement:

As you approach the climax, explore the entire fretboard. Move towards higher registers, utilize higher positions on the neck, and experiment with arpeggios or scale runs that cover a broader range. This expansive movement adds a sense of grandeur to the melodic development.

Delayed Resolution:

Delay the resolution. Just before reaching the climactic point, introduce a moment of suspension or hesitation. This brief delay heightens the emotional impact when the resolution finally occurs, creating a more pronounced sense of release.

Examples from Popular Music:

Stairway to Heaven by Led Zeppelin:
The iconic solo in *Stairway to Heaven* builds towards an emotional climax. Jimmy Page gradually increases the intensity of his melodic phrases, incorporating higher notes, dynamic picking, and expressive bends before reaching the peak of the solo.

Bohemian Rhapsody by Queen:
The operatic section of *Bohemian Rhapsody* is a masterclass in building towards climaxes. Freddie Mercury's vocal lines progressively intensify, leading to the powerful and emotive peak of the song.

High Hopes by Pink Floyd:
In the solo of *High Hopes*, David Gilmour builds melodic phrases towards a climactic point through strategic note selection, expressive bends, and a gradual increase in dynamic intensity.

Eruption by Van Halen:
Eddie Van Halen's guitar solo in *Eruption* is an example of explosive climactic development. The solo begins with a restrained tapping motif and gradually

builds towards a virtuosic climax, showcasing fretboard mastery and emotional intensity.

Incorporating these techniques into your guitar composition allows you to craft melodic phrases that lead the listener on a compelling journey. By strategically building towards climaxes, you create moments of heightened emotion and impact, leaving a lasting impression on your audience. Experiment with these approaches and adapt them to your own style and musical context.

MELODIC INVERSIONS

Try inverting or reversing certain melodic motifs. This can provide a fresh perspective and add complexity to your phrases.

EXPERIMENTING WITH MELODIC INVERSIONS

Melodic inversions in guitar composition involve reversing or flipping certain melodic motifs to create variations in the musical theme. By inverting melodies, you can bring a fresh perspective to your composition, offering a new sonic angle while maintaining a connection to the original motif.

Below, we delve into what melodic inversions are and explore how to apply them in guitar composition.

UNDERSTANDING MELODIC INVERSIONS

Inversion is a technique where the pitch order of a melodic motif is reversed. This means that ascending intervals become descending, and vice versa. In the context of guitar composition, this can be applied to phrases, scales, arpeggios, or any sequence of notes. Inverting a melodic motif adds variety, complexity, and a sense of exploration to your musical ideas.

HOW TO APPLY MELODIC INVERSIONS

Identify a Melodic Motif:
Begin with a melodic motif that you want to invert. This could be a short phrase, a scale fragment, or an arpeggio. The motif should be distinctive enough to be recognizable when inverted.

Determine the Axis of Inversion:

Choose an axis or pivot point around which you will invert the motif. This axis can be a specific note within the motif or a central point within the overall melody.

Reverse the Order of Pitches:

Invert the pitches of the motif by reversing their order. If a note is higher than the axis in the original motif, it becomes lower in the inverted version, and vice versa.

Maintain Rhythmic Integrity:

While inverting pitches, maintain the rhythmic integrity of the original motif. The inverted version should have the same rhythmic structure as the original, ensuring a seamless transition between the two.

EXPERIMENT WITH VARIATIONS

Explore different inversion possibilities. You can experiment with inverting only certain portions of the motif, creating variations that maintain a balance between familiarity and novelty.

Examples of Melodic Inversions:

Inverted Arpeggio:

Original Motif: C - E - G

Inverted Motif: G - E - C

Apply inversion to a simple arpeggio, such as a C major triad. The inverted version maintains the same notes but presents them in a reversed order.

Inverted Scale Fragment:

Original Motif: A - B - C - D - E

Inverted Motif: E - D - C - B - A

Apply inversion to a ascending scale fragment. The inversion results in a descending scale, offering a contrasting perspective.

Inverted Melodic Phrase:

Original Motif: G - A - B - G

Inverted Motif: G - B - A - G

Invert a short melodic phrase, creating a variation that maintains the contour of the original but introduces a different harmonic and emotional flavor.

Inverted Chord Progression:

Original Motif: Dm - G - C

Inverted Motif: C - G - Dm

Apply inversion to a chord progression. The inverted version preserves the harmonic relationships but introduces a sense of unpredictability.

BENEFITS OF MELODIC INVERSIONS

Variety and Interest:

Melodic inversions introduce variety and interest to your composition, preventing it from sounding predictable or repetitive.

Development of Musical Themes:

Inverting motifs allows you to develop and explore musical themes in different directions, contributing to the overall evolution of your composition.

Enhanced Creativity:

Experimenting with melodic inversions stimulates creativity, encouraging you to view familiar motifs from different angles and discover new possibilities.

Incorporating melodic inversions into your guitar composition is a powerful way to add depth, complexity, and intrigue. By flipping and reversing motifs, you breathe new life into familiar musical ideas, inviting listeners to experience your composition from fresh perspectives. Experiment with melodic inversions to unlock the creative potential within your guitar compositions.

RECORD AND LISTEN

Record your playing and actively listen to the recorded phrases. This allows you to objectively assess the development of your melody and make refinements.

RECORDING AND ACTIVE LISTENING

Recording your playing and actively listening to the recorded phrases is an indispensable practice for successful guitar composition. This process serves as a valuable tool for refining your melodic development, honing your skills, and elevating the overall quality of your compositions.

Objective Self-Evaluation:

Recording allows you to step back and objectively evaluate your playing. When you're in the moment of creation, it's easy to get caught up in the emotion and nuances of the performance. Listening to a recorded version provides a more detached perspective, helping you identify areas for improvement and refinement.

Capturing Spontaneity and Inspiration:

Inspiration often strikes in spontaneous moments, and some of your best musical ideas may emerge during improvisation or casual playing. Recording ensures that you capture these moments, preserving the spontaneity and authenticity of your playing. This can lead to the discovery of unique and compelling melodic ideas that might be lost if not recorded.

Iterative Refinement:

Successful guitar composition often involves an iterative process of refinement. By recording and listening, you can identify specific elements in your melodic development that work well and those that may need adjustment. This iterative refinement is crucial for crafting a melody that truly resonates with your creative vision.

Improved Timing and Rhythm:

Recording helps you focus on your timing and rhythm. It allows you to pinpoint any inconsistencies or areas where your rhythmic execution may need attention. Tightening up your timing enhances the overall groove and feel of your melodic phrases, contributing to a more polished composition.

Enhanced Musical Memory:

Actively listening to recorded phrases contributes to the development of your musical memory. It reinforces the melodic ideas in your mind, making it easier to recall and integrate them into your compositions. This process aids in the creation of cohesive and memorable musical narratives.

Analyzing Dynamics and Expression:

Recording reveals nuances in dynamics and expression that may be overlooked during live playing. By actively listening, you can analyze how subtle variations in dynamics, articulation, and expression contribute to the emotional impact of your melodic phrases. This insight enables you to refine and enhance these elements deliberately.

Feedback and Collaboration:

Recording facilitates feedback from others, whether it's from bandmates, peers, or mentors. Sharing your recorded compositions opens the door for constructive input, fresh perspectives, and collaborative opportunities. The feedback you receive can be invaluable in refining your melodic development and elevating your composition to new heights.

Documenting Progress:

Recording serves as a documented record of your progress as a guitarist and composer. Listening back to earlier recordings allows you to track your growth, identify patterns in your playing style, and celebrate milestones achieved along your musical journey.

In the realm of guitar composition, recording and active listening form a dynamic duo that propels your creativity forward. These practices provide a mirror for self-reflection, a repository for spontaneous brilliance, and a platform for collaborative exploration. Embrace the habit of recording your playing, actively listen to the recorded phrases, and witness the transformative impact on your melodic development and overall guitar composition skills.

ROLE OF OTHER MUSICIANS

Listen to a variety of music and study how other musicians develop their melodic ideas. Analyze their techniques and adapt them to your own style.

SEEK INSPIRATION FROM OTHER MUSICIANS

Analyzing other musicians' techniques and adapting them to your own style is a powerful approach to melodically developing your guitar composition. By studying the work of accomplished guitarists, you gain insights into various melodic strategies, stylistic nuances, and expressive techniques.

We can learn how to effectively analyze and integrate these influences into your own musical vocabulary below.

Select Influential Musicians:

Identify guitarists who inspire you or align with the style you want to incorporate into your composition. This could range from legendary figures to contemporary artists. Choose musicians whose techniques resonate with your musical goals.

Break Down Melodic Structures:

Listen closely to the melodic structures employed by your chosen musicians. Break down their solos, riffs, or compositions into smaller components. Identify recurring motifs, scales, arpeggios, and rhythmic patterns. Understanding the building blocks of their melodies is crucial for adapting these elements to your own style.

Study Articulation and Phrasing:

Pay attention to the articulation and phrasing techniques used by the musicians you're analyzing. Notice how they employ bends, slides, hammer-ons, pull-offs, and vibrato to add expressiveness to their playing. Analyzing these nuances will enable you to incorporate similar techniques into your own melodic development.

Explore Unique Scale Choices:

Investigate the scales and modes favored by your chosen musicians. Whether it's the bluesy pentatonic scales, exotic modes, or jazz-influenced harmonic choices, understanding their scale preferences provides you with a broader palette of melodic options to explore in your composition.

Emulate Rhythmic Variations:

Focus on the rhythmic variations present in their playing. Experiment with syncopations, accents, and unusual rhythmic groupings. Emulating these rhythmic elements can add a dynamic and unpredictable quality to your own melodic ideas.

Analyze Harmonic Progressions:

Explore the harmonic progressions used in their compositions. Understand how they navigate chord changes, introduce tension, and create resolution. This analysis is crucial for incorporating harmonic richness into your own melodic development.

Experiment with Dynamics:

Note how your selected musicians utilize dynamics to convey emotion and intensity. Experiment with variations in volume, attack, and release in your playing. Dynamic control is a powerful tool for shaping the emotional arc of your melodic phrases.

Integrate Fingerboard Techniques:

Examine fingerboard techniques specific to your chosen musicians, such as tapping, sweeping, or fingerstyle techniques. Integrate these techniques into your practice routine, gradually incorporating them into your melodic development as they become more familiar.

Personalize and Combine Ideas:

Once you've analyzed and practiced various techniques, personalize them by incorporating your own creative twists. Don't merely replicate; strive to make these techniques an organic part of your playing style. Experiment with combining ideas from different musicians to create a unique blend that reflects your individuality.

Continual Self-Assessment:

Regularly assess your progress and the integration of these techniques into your own style. Listen critically to recordings of your playing, seeking areas where your adaptation of these influences shines and areas for further refinement.

Examples:

Jimi Hendrix's Innovative Chord Voicings:
Analyze Hendrix's use of innovative chord voicings and incorporate them into your rhythm and lead playing.

David Gilmour's Bending and Vibrato Techniques:
Study Gilmour's expressive bending and vibrato techniques, applying them to your own solos for added emotion.

John Mayer's Bluesy Phrasing:
Explore Mayer's bluesy phrasing and incorporate similar sliding, bending, and dynamic techniques into your melodic development.

Analyzing other musicians' techniques is a rich source of inspiration and a catalyst for personal growth as a guitarist and composer. By understanding the intricacies of their melodic choices, you not only expand your technical repertoire but also deepen your understanding of musical expression.

The key lies in adapting these influences authentically to your own style, creating a fusion that is uniquely yours. Embrace the journey of continuous learning and experimentation as you integrate diverse melodic elements into your guitar composition.

SPONTANEITY

Allow for moments of spontaneity and improvisation during the development process. Sometimes, the most captivating phrases emerge when you follow your instincts.

SPONTANEITY AND IMPROVISATION

Embracing spontaneity and improvisation during the melodic development process of guitar composition can lead to fresh, dynamic, and authentic musical expressions. These elements infuse your composition with a sense of vitality, allowing your creativity to flow freely and yielding unique melodic ideas.

Below, we lay out some ways to incorporate spontaneity and improvisation into your guitar composition.

Create a Playful Atmosphere:

Establish a playful and open-minded mindset before diving into your melodic development. Encourage yourself to explore and experiment without the constraints of preconceived notions. This sets the stage for spontaneity to thrive.

Start with a Blank Canvas:

Begin with a blank musical canvas. Instead of adhering to a rigid structure or predefined melody, let your fingers explore the fretboard without specific expectations. Allow the initial moments of your composition to unfold organically.

Use Jamming Sessions:

Engage in jamming sessions, whether with other musicians or by using backing tracks. These sessions provide a supportive environment for spontaneous improvisation. Respond to the musical context in real-time, allowing your melodic ideas to emerge naturally.

Leverage Scales and Modes:

Familiarize yourself with scales and modes, as they serve as the foundation for spontaneous improvisation. Experiment with different scales to evoke various moods and emotions. For example, shifting between the major and minor pentatonic scales can create contrasting tonalities.

Employ Call-and-Response Techniques:

Incorporate call-and-response techniques into your improvisation. Play a short melodic phrase and respond to it with another. This dialogical approach adds a conversational and interactive element to your spontaneous musical expressions.

Examples of Spontaneity and Improvisation:

Jimi Hendrix's *Purple Haze* Solo:
Hendrix was renowned for his spontaneous and innovative approach to guitar playing. In the solo of *Purple Haze*, he incorporates unconventional bends, feedback, and expressive phrasing. The entire solo feels like a spontaneous outpouring of creative energy.

Carlos Santana's Improvised Sections:

Santana often incorporates spontaneous improvisation in his guitar solos. In tracks like *Black Magic Woman*, his solos feel like fluid, evolving conversations with the underlying musical backdrop, showcasing the power of improvisation in melodic development.

John Mayer's Live Performances:

John Mayer is known for his dynamic improvisational skills during live performances. In songs like *Gravity*, he often extends guitar solos, exploring different melodic avenues. Mayer's ability to spontaneously develop melodic ideas contributes to the vibrancy of his live renditions.

Capture Moments of Inspiration:

Keep recording devices or apps handy during your playing sessions. When you stumble upon a spontaneous and inspiring melodic idea, capture it immediately. These impromptu moments can become valuable building blocks for your composition.

Embrace "Mistakes" as Opportunities:

View unexpected notes or "mistakes" as opportunities for new melodic directions. Often, these spontaneous deviations from your original plan lead to innovative and unexpected musical discoveries.

Develop Repetitive Patterns:

As you improvise, identify melodic patterns that resonate with you. Repetition of these patterns can create a sense of continuity and familiarity within your composition, providing cohesion amidst spontaneity.

Mix Techniques and Dynamics:

Experiment with a variety of techniques and dynamics during your improvisation. Combine picking styles, incorporate slides, utilize fingerstyle, and explore different levels of volume and intensity. This multidimensional approach adds texture and depth to your melodic ideas.

Allow for Silence and Space:

Embrace moments of silence and space within your improvisation. Pauses can be as impactful as notes, providing contrast and allowing listeners to absorb the nuances of your spontaneous melodic expressions.

Incorporating spontaneity and improvisation into your melodic development process not only enhances the creativity of your guitar composition but also fosters a deeper connection between you and your instrument. By allowing your musical ideas to unfold organically, you infuse your composition with a genuine, living quality. Experiment with these techniques, embrace the unpredictability of improvisation, and let your creativity soar as you navigate the uncharted territories of spontaneous melodic development on the guitar.

ITERATION

Iterate on your melodic ideas and phrases. Refinement is an ongoing process that leads to the crystallization of your musical vision.

HOW TO ITERATE AND REFINE

Iterating on your melodic ideas and phrases is a crucial step in the creative process of guitar composition. It involves exploring various possibilities, experimenting with different elements, and refining your initial concepts to achieve a more polished and expressive result.

Capture Initial Ideas:

Begin by capturing your initial melodic ideas as they spontaneously arise. Record them, write them down, or use notation software to document the essence of your inspiration.

Experiment with Variations:

Once you have your initial ideas, start experimenting with variations. Change the rhythm, try different articulations, explore alternative note sequences, or experiment with dynamic variations. This phase is about expanding the possibilities of your original concept.

Play with Harmony:

Explore how your melodic ideas interact with different harmonies. Experiment with chord progressions and identify how alterations in harmony impact the emotional character of your melody. This can lead to new directions and possibilities.

Incorporate Articulation Techniques:

Introduce various articulation techniques, such as slides, bends, hammer-ons, and pull-offs. Experiment with how these techniques can add nuance and character to your melodic phrases.

Dynamic Experimentation:

Play with dynamic variations. Experiment with loud and soft sections, create crescendos and decrescendos, and explore how changes in dynamics contribute to the overall expressiveness of your melody.

Iterate in Different Registers:

Explore how your melodic ideas sound in different registers of the guitar. Moving between high and low registers can create interesting contrasts and add dimension to your composition.

Combine Melodic Fragments:

Experiment with combining different melodic fragments. You might find that elements from separate ideas complement each other, leading to the creation of a more intricate and cohesive melody.

Listen Critically:

Take the time to listen critically to your explorations. Identify what elements resonate with you and contribute positively to the mood and narrative of your composition.

REFINEMENT PROCESS

Select the Strongest Elements:

Identify the strongest elements that emerged during your experimentation. These could be particular melodic fragments, harmonies, or articulation techniques that stand out.

Streamline and Simplify:

Streamline your melodic ideas by simplifying and focusing on the core elements that make the composition compelling. Avoid overcrowding the melody with excessive ornamentation.

Ensure Logical Progression:

Ensure that your melodic ideas flow logically. Evaluate the transitions between different phrases and make sure there is a coherent progression that engages the listener.

Fine-Tune Rhythmic Elements:

Fine-tune the rhythmic elements of your melody. Ensure that the rhythm complements the mood you want to convey and that it contributes to the overall groove and feel of the composition.

Polish Articulation and Dynamics:

Polish the articulation and dynamics of your melodic phrases. Ensure that articulation techniques are executed precisely, and dynamic variations contribute to the expressiveness of the composition.

Check for Guitaristic Playability:

Consider the playability on the guitar. Verify that the fingerings are comfortable, and the transitions between notes and chords are smooth. This step is essential for ensuring that your composition is feasible for live performance.

Seek Feedback:

Share your refined melodic ideas with trusted peers, mentors, or fellow musicians. Seek constructive feedback to gain insights from fresh perspectives and refine further based on valuable input.

Final Recording:

Once you're satisfied with the refined version of your melodic composition, create a final recording. This could be a high-quality audio recording or a notation file, depending on your preference.

Iterating on your melodic ideas and refining them for guitar composition is a dynamic and iterative process. Embrace experimentation, be open to exploring different possibilities, and refine with a discerning ear. This iterative cycle of exploration and refinement is the key to unlocking the full potential of your melodic creativity on the guitar.

COMPLEXITY AND SIMPLICITY

Strike a balance between complexity and simplicity. While embellishments and variations are valuable, simplicity can be equally powerful and memorable.

BALANCE COMPLEXITY AND SIMPLICITY

Striking a balance between complexity and simplicity is an art that can greatly influence the effectiveness and accessibility of your melodic development in guitar compositions. Finding the right equilibrium allows you to create engaging and memorable melodies while avoiding the pitfalls of either overwhelming complexity or monotony.

Let's dive into learning how to achieve the beautiful balance.

Start with a Strong Core:

Complexity: Begin with a simple and strong core melody.

Simplicity: Avoid excessive embellishments at the initial stage.

Example:

Original Phrase: A straightforward descending scale.

Complex Variation: Introduce rhythmic variations without adding extra notes.

Layer Complexity Gradually:

Complexity: Add layers of complexity progressively as the melody unfolds.

Simplicity: Begin with a straightforward presentation.

Example:

Initial Phrase: Simple arpeggio.

Layered Complexity: Introduce additional notes or harmonies in subsequent repetitions.

Dynamic Contrast:

Complexity: Experiment with intricate phrases for dynamic sections.

Simplicity: Use simpler motifs for calmer sections.

Example:

Complex Section: Ornate melodic run during a climax.

Simple Section: Unadorned chords during a softer passage.

Focus on Key Elements:

Complexity: Highlight key elements with embellishments.

Simplicity: Allow key elements to stand out without overshadowing the overall melody.

Example:

Key Element: A distinctive interval leap.

Complex Variation: Introduce ornamentation while preserving the integrity of the leap.

Rhythmic Variations:

Complexity: Introduce intricate rhythms for added interest.

Simplicity: Start with a straightforward rhythmic pattern.

Example:

Simple Rhythm: Basic quarter and eighth notes.

Complex Rhythm: Syncopated patterns or irregular groupings.

Harmonic Variations:

Complexity: Experiment with complex harmonies.

Simplicity: Begin with a straightforward chord progression.

Example:

Simple Harmonic Progression: Basic I–IV–V progression.

Complex Variation: Incorporate extended chords or modal interchange.

Silence as a Tool:

Complexity: Use moments of silence strategically for contrast.

Simplicity: Allow sustained notes or simple phrases to breathe.

Example:

Complex Section: Quick, staccato bursts with pauses.

Simple Section: Smooth legato phrases with fewer breaks.

Vary Texture:

Complexity: Experiment with thick textures using multiple voices.

Simplicity: Embrace simplicity by focusing on single-note lines.

Example:

Complex Texture: Double-stops, triads, or arpeggios.

Simple Texture: Single-note melody with minimal harmonic support.

Embrace Restraint:

Complexity: Display technical prowess selectively.

Simplicity: Embrace restraint in certain sections.

Example:

Complex Section: Fast, intricate picking or tapping.

Simple Section: Sparse, deliberate note choices.

Listen and Assess:

Complexity: Be attentive to the overall feel and listener experience.

Simplicity: Gauge if the complexity serves the emotional context.

Example:

Complex Section: Evaluate if technical intricacies enhance or distract from the intended mood.

Simple Section: Ensure that simplicity doesn't compromise engagement.

Achieving a balance between complexity and simplicity in melodic development for guitar compositions is an ongoing process of refinement and self-awareness. By strategically incorporating elements of both, you create compositions that captivate the listener's attention while maintaining accessibility. Experiment with these principles, adapt them to your style, and let the interplay between complexity and simplicity be a dynamic force in shaping the character and impact of your guitar melodies.

FEEDBACK

Share your developing melodic ideas with others and seek constructive feedback. External perspectives can offer valuable insights and suggestions for improvement.

QUESTIONS TO INCORPORATE FEEDBACK

When sharing your developing melodic ideas with others and seeking constructive feedback, asking the right questions is crucial to receive insightful and actionable responses.

Overall Impression:

1. What is your overall impression of the melody?
2. Does the melody evoke a specific mood or emotion?

Memorability:

1. Is the melody memorable? Does it linger in your mind after listening?
2. Are there specific parts of the melody that stand out to you?

Clarity and Cohesion:

1. Is the melodic development clear and cohesive, or are there moments that feel disjointed?
2. How well do the different sections flow into each other?

Instrumentation and Arrangement:

1. How does the melody interact with the chosen instrumentation or arrangement?
2. Are there suggestions for additional instrumentation or arrangement tweaks?

Dynamic Range:

1. Does the melody have a good dynamic range? Are there moments of contrast in terms of volume and intensity?
2. Can you identify sections where dynamic variations could be enhanced?

Rhythmic Elements:

1. How effective are the rhythmic elements in the melody?
2. Are there specific rhythmic patterns that work well or could be improved?

Harmonic Structure:

1. How do you perceive the harmonic structure of the melody?
2. Are there harmonic choices that stand out positively or require adjustments?

Use of Articulation and Techniques:

1. How do articulation techniques (e.g., bends, slides, hammer-ons) contribute to the expressiveness of the melody?
2. Are there specific techniques that could be emphasized or refined?

Pacing and Momentum:

1. How is the pacing of the melody? Does it maintain a compelling momentum?
2. Are there sections where the pacing could be adjusted for better overall flow?

Emotional Impact:

1. Does the melody convey the intended emotions or mood?
2. Are there areas where the emotional impact could be heightened or clarified?

Fingerings and Playability:

1. From a guitarist's perspective, are the fingerings comfortable and practical?
2. Are there sections that might be challenging to play smoothly?

Suggestions for Improvement:

1. Based on your listening experience, what specific suggestions do you have for improvement?
2. Are there any elements that you think could be enhanced or explored further?

Comparisons and Influences:

1. Does the melody remind you of any other compositions or artists?
2. Are there specific influences that you think could be incorporated or diverged from?

Audience Perspective:

1. How do you think the melody would resonate with a broader audience?

2. Are there adjustments that could make the melody more universally appealing?

Encourage Specific Feedback:

Ask for specific feedback on particular sections or aspects that you find challenging or uncertain about.

Remember to create an open and comfortable environment for feedback, emphasizing that constructive criticism is welcomed. Encourage honesty and diverse perspectives to gain a well-rounded understanding of how your melodic ideas are being perceived.

BLUEPRINT FOR GUITAR MELODY

Before adding harmonies, thoroughly understand the structure and nuances of your melody. Identify key notes, phrases, and emotional elements that you want to highlight.

CREATING A MELODIC BLUEPRINT

Creating a blueprint for the structure and nuances of your melody is a crucial step in shaping a compelling guitar composition. This blueprint will help you identify key elements such as notes, phrases, and emotional nuances.

Let's look at the following detailed information to learn how to create an effective melodic blueprint for stunning guitar compositions.

BLUEPRINT FOR GUITAR MELODY

Identify Key Notes and Scale:
1. Choose a specific scale that suits the mood of your composition.
2. Identify the key notes within the scale that will serve as anchor points for your melody.

Define Phrases:
1. Divide your melody into distinct phrases, each with its own musical idea.
2. Consider the balance between repetition and variation in connecting these phrases.

Emotional Mapping:

1. Assign emotions or moods to different sections of your melody.
2. Consider the emotional journey you want to take the listener on and how each phrase contributes to that narrative.

Dynamic Structure:

1. Plan the dynamic structure of your melody. Identify where you want peaks, valleys, and moments of intensity.
2. Determine the overall dynamic arc of the melody, considering crescendos, decrescendos, and dynamic contrasts.

Articulation Techniques:

1. Integrate articulation techniques strategically throughout the melody.
2. Identify specific points where techniques like bends, slides, or hammer-ons can add expressiveness.

Rhythmic Patterns:

1. Define rhythmic patterns for each phrase. Consider variations to maintain interest.
2. Explore syncopation, different time signatures, or rhythmic motifs to add complexity.

Harmonic Progression:

1. Outline the harmonic progression that accompanies your melody.

2. Identify chord changes and their relationship to key notes in each phrase.

Melodic Arcs and Contours:
1. Analyze the melodic arcs and contours within phrases.
2. Ensure a balance between ascending and descending lines, and consider leaps for dramatic effect.

Use of Space and Silence:
1. Strategically incorporate moments of space and silence.
2. Allow certain notes or phrases to breathe, creating a sense of anticipation and contrast.

Fingerboard Positioning:
1. Plan the positioning of your melody on the guitar fretboard.
2. Consider the tonal qualities of different positions and how they contribute to the overall texture.

Transitions Between Phrases:
1. Focus on smooth transitions between phrases.
2. Use transitional elements, such as connecting notes or slides, to ensure a cohesive flow.

Key Changes or Modulations:
1. Determine if and where key changes or modulations might enhance the melodic development.
2. Experiment with transitions between different keys for added interest.

Repetition and Variation:

1. Strategically use repetition within phrases for cohesion.
2. Introduce variation to maintain listener engagement and prevent predictability.

Pitch Bend and Vibrato Usage:

1. Plan for the use of pitch bends and vibrato to add character.
2. Identify specific notes or phrases where these techniques can enhance expressiveness.

Melody as a Vocal Line:

1. Imagine your melody as a vocal line. Consider how a singer might interpret and phrase the melody.
2. Mimic the ebb and flow of natural vocal expression.

Audience Connection:

1. Assess how your melody might connect with your target audience.
2. Consider the impact of your melody on the listener and make adjustments to align with your artistic vision.

This detailed blueprint serves as a roadmap for your guitar melody, guiding you through the intricacies of structure, emotion, and expression. Use it as a flexible guide, allowing room for creativity and adjustments as you bring your melody to life. Regularly revisit and refine the blueprint as your composition evolves, ensuring that it aligns with the emotive and artistic goals you've set for your guitar composition.

SAMPLE MELODIC BLUEPRINT

Let's create a sample blueprint for a guitar melody. For the sake of this example, let's consider a melody in the key of A minor with a contemplative and introspective mood.

EXAMPLE BLUEPRINT FOR GUITAR MELODY IN A MINOR

Identify Key Notes and Scale:

Scale: A Natural Minor

Key Notes: A, B, C, D, E, F, G

Define Phrases:

Phrase 1: Ascending sequence emphasizing A, B, and C.

Phrase 2: Descending arpeggio featuring G, E, and A.

Phrase 3: Repetition of Phrase 1 with slight variations.

Phrase 4: Climactic leap to high E followed by a gentle descent.

Emotional Mapping:

Phrase 1: Introduce a sense of curiosity and exploration.

Phrase 2: Convey introspection and a touch of melancholy.

Phrase 3: Develop a feeling of familiarity and comfort.

Phrase 4: Build towards a moment of resolution and emotional release.

Dynamic Structure:

Overall Arc: Gradual rise in dynamics, peaking in Phrase

Specific Dynamics: Subtle dynamics in Phrases 1 and 3; Increase intensity in Phrases 2 and

Articulation Techniques:

Phrase 1: Incorporate gentle hammer-ons for a smooth flow.

Phrase 2: Use expressive vibrato on sustained notes.

Phrase 3: Experiment with slides for a warm and connected feel.

Phrase 4: Introduce a subtle pitch bend for added emotion.

Rhythmic Patterns:

Phrase 1: Simple quarter and eighth note patterns.

Phrase 2: Explore triplet rhythms for added complexity.

Phrase 3: Maintain a steady rhythm with occasional syncopation.

Phrase 4: Use sustained notes and pauses for dramatic effect.

Harmonic Progression:

Chords: Em, Dm, G, Am, F, E.

Phrase 2: Emphasize Dm and G for a contemplative feel.

Phrase 4: Introduce a brief modulation to C major for resolution.

Melodic Arcs and Contours:

Ascending Motion: In Phrases 1 and 3 for a sense of optimism.

Descending Motion: In Phrases 2 and 4 to convey introspection and resolution.

Leaps: Strategically placed to add interest and emotion.

Use of Space and Silence:

Space: Introduce pauses after the climactic points in Phrases 2 and

Silence: Allow for brief moments of silence for emotional impact.

Fingerboard Positioning:

Phrase 1 and 3: Centered around the middle of the fretboard.

Phrase 2: Explores lower register for a deeper, introspective tone.

Phrase 4: Moves to higher positions for a sense of elevation.

Transitions Between Phrases:

Transitional Elements: Slides and gentle transitions between phrases for cohesion.

Key Changes or Modulations:

Brief Modulation: Transition from A minor to C major in Phrase 4 for resolution.

Repetition and Variation:

Repetition: Revisit elements of Phrases 1 and 3 for continuity.

Variation: Introduce nuanced variations in each repetition for sustained interest.

Pitch Bend and Vibrato Usage:

Vibrato: Applied on sustained notes in Phrases 2 and

Pitch Bend: Subtle bend at the peak of Phrase 4 for expressive impact.

Melody as a Vocal Line:

Imagined Vocal Quality: Gentle and reflective, akin to a singer conveying personal thoughts.

Audience Connection:

Intended Reaction: A sense of introspection, followed by emotional release and resolution.

Adjustments: Make adjustments to enhance emotional connection without compromising artistic intent.

This blueprint serves as a guide for developing a guitar melody with specific attention to key notes, phrases, and emotional elements. Feel free to adapt and modify elements based on your preferences and the specific mood you want to convey in your composition. This blueprint provides a structured foundation while leaving room for artistic expression and exploration.

The process of developing melody is both an art and a craft. Trust your creative instincts, be open to exploration, and enjoy the journey of sculpting your initial ideas into cohesive and expressive phrases for your guitar composition.

HARMONY DEVELOPMENT

Exploring harmonies that complement your melody is a fantastic way to enrich the sonic landscape of your guitar composition. Harmonies can add depth, emotion, and complexity to your music. Here's a guide on how to explore harmonies that enhance and complement your melody in guitar composition:

IDENTIFY CHORD PROGRESSIONS

Analyze the underlying chord progressions that support your melody. Knowing the chords provides a foundation for creating harmonies that align with the harmonic context of your composition.

ANALYZING CHORD PROGRESSIONS

Analyzing the underlying chord progressions that support your melody is a crucial step in creating harmonies for your guitar composition. Harmonies provide a rich and supportive backdrop to your melody, enhancing its emotional impact and adding depth to the overall musical experience.

Identify the Chord Progression:
1. Examine the existing chord progression that accompanies your melody.
2. Determine the chords played at each point in your melody, including any changes or variations.

Harmonic Analysis:

1. Break down the harmonic function of each chord (e.g., tonic, subdominant, dominant).
2. Identify any non-diatonic or borrowed chords that contribute to the overall harmonic palette.

Determine Chord Quality:

1. Establish the quality of each chord (major, minor, dominant, diminished, etc.).
2. Pay attention to the emotional nuances conveyed by different chord qualities.

Explore Inversions:

1. Consider inversions of the chords to add variety and smooth voice leading.
2. Experiment with different voicings to find harmonic structures that complement the melody.

Voice Leading:

1. Analyze the voice leading between chords to ensure smooth transitions.
2. Aim for stepwise motion or common tones between chords for a connected harmonic flow.

Add Seventh or Extended Chords:

1. Experiment with adding seventh chords or extended harmonies for a more sophisticated sound.
2. Determine which extended chords align with the emotional character of your melody.

Secondary Dominants:
1. Identify opportunities to introduce secondary dominants for heightened tension and resolution.
2. Use secondary dominants to temporarily shift the tonal center and add interest.

Modal Borrowing:
1. Explore modal borrowing by incorporating chords from parallel modes.
2. Consider how modal interchange can introduce unique colors to your harmonies.

Rhythmic Emphasis:
1. Align chord changes with rhythmic accents in your melody.
2. Experiment with syncopated or anticipatory chord changes for rhythmic interest.

Cadences:
1. Identify cadences within the chord progression (e.g., authentic, plagal, deceptive).
2. Use cadences to punctuate phrases and contribute to the overall structure.

Create Harmonic Variations:
1. Experiment with creating harmonic variations within the chord progression.
2. Consider alternative progressions that maintain a sense of coherence while offering a fresh perspective.

Consider Melody Notes as Chord Tones:

1. Treat prominent melody notes as chord tones within the accompanying harmony.
2. Ensure that these melody notes align with the underlying chord to enhance harmonic unity.

Build a Harmonic Rhythm:

1. Establish a harmonic rhythm that complements the pacing of your melody.
2. Vary the duration of each chord to create interest and emphasize certain moments.

Chord Transitions and Modulations:

1. Smoothly transition between chords using common tones or pivot chords.
2. Explore subtle modulations to related keys for dynamic shifts in mood.

Evaluate Emotional Impact:

1. Assess how different harmonies contribute to the emotional impact of your melody.
2. Make adjustments to harmonies that align more closely with the intended emotional expression.

Recording and Listening:

1. Record your harmonized melody and actively listen to the interplay between melody and harmony.
2. Identify sections where harmonies enhance or potentially overshadow the melody.

Analyzing chord progressions and creating harmonies is a meticulous process that significantly influences the character of your guitar composition. Strive for a harmonically rich backdrop that supports and elevates your melody, creating a cohesive musical experience for the listener. Through careful analysis and creative exploration, you can craft harmonies that resonate with the emotional depth of your melody and enhance the overall impact of your guitar composition.

SEEK INSPIRATION

Listen to compositions in various genres and study how harmonies are used to enhance melodies. Draw inspiration from different styles and adapt ideas to your own guitar composition.

QUESTIONS TO GUIDE YOU

When listening to compositions across various genres to study how harmonies enhance melodies in guitar composition, it's essential to approach the analysis with a curious and attentive mindset.

How are Chords Voiced?

Pay attention to the arrangement of notes within chords. Are they spread out or closely voiced? How does voicing contribute to the overall harmonic texture?

What is the Role of Suspensions and Resolutions?

Identify moments of tension and release within the harmonies. How are suspensions used, and how do they resolve? How does this impact the emotional feel of the composition?

Are There Modal Elements?

Determine if the composition incorporates modal elements. Are there borrowed chords from related modes? How does modal interchange contribute to the overall harmonic palette?

How Do Harmonies Support the Melodic Phrasing?

Analyze how harmonies complement and support the contours of the melody. Do harmonic changes coincide with melodic peaks or valleys?

Are There Pedal Tones or Drones?

Explore if the composition uses pedal tones or sustained drones. How do these elements interact with the melodic lines, and what impact do they have on the overall harmonic atmosphere?

What Role Does Counterpoint Play?

Consider instances of counterpoint within the harmonies. How are multiple melodic lines interacting, and how does this contribute to the overall complexity of the composition?

Is There a Dominant-Tonic Relationship?

Identify instances of dominant and tonic chords. How is the dominant-tonic relationship used to create tension and resolution within the composition?

How Do Harmonies Change in Different Sections?

Observe how harmonies evolve throughout different sections of the composition. Are there key changes or shifts in harmonic complexity? How do these changes contribute to the overall structure?

Are There Unusual or Unique Harmonic Progressions?

Look for unexpected or unconventional harmonic progressions. How do these departures from typical progressions impact the listener's experience?

What Role Do Seventh, Ninth, or Extended Chords Play?

Explore the use of extended chords. How are seventh, ninth, or other extended chords used to add color and complexity to the harmonic palette?

How Does Rhythm Influence Harmonic Progression?

Consider the relationship between rhythm and harmonic progression. How do rhythmic changes influence the timing of harmonic shifts?

Are There Instances of Chromaticism?

Identify moments of chromaticism within the harmonies. How are chromatic elements used to add tension, and how do they resolve?

Does the Composition Use Harmonic Embellishments?

Pay attention to any embellishments within the harmonies. Are there grace notes, slides, or other embellishments that enhance the expressiveness of the harmonies?

How Do Harmonies Contribute to the Overall Mood?

Consider the emotional impact of the harmonies. How do they contribute to the mood and atmosphere of the composition? How does harmony enhance the intended emotional message?

Is There Interplay Between Harmony and Melodic Technique?

Examine the relationship between harmony and melodic techniques. How do techniques like bends, slides, or vibrato interact with the underlying harmonies?

How Does the Use of Space Impact Harmonic Perception?

Consider moments of silence or sparse harmonic arrangements. How does the use of space impact the listener's perception of the harmonies and melodies?

What is the Role of Dynamic Changes in Harmonies?

Explore how dynamic changes within the harmonies contribute to the overall dynamics of the composition. How do changes in volume or intensity enhance the harmonic progression?

Are There Examples of Harmonic Sequences?

Look for instances of harmonic sequences. How are sequences used to create patterns or motifs within the composition?

As you listen and study compositions across various genres, these questions will help you deepen your understanding of how harmonies interact with melodies in guitar composition. Keep in mind that each genre may have unique conventions and approaches, so adapt your analysis accordingly.

PREDICTABILITY AND SURPRISE

Strike a balance between predictable harmonies that provide stability and surprising harmonies that capture attention. The interplay between the expected and unexpected keeps the listener engaged.

BALANCING PREDICTABILITY AND SURPRISE

Balancing predictability and surprise in developing harmonies for guitar composition is an art that involves engaging your audience with familiar elements while introducing unexpected twists to maintain interest. Striking this balance creates a dynamic and engaging listening experience.

Establish a Harmonic Foundation:

Begin with a solid harmonic foundation based on the key and tonal center of your composition. This provides a sense of predictability and stability.

Use Conventional Progressions Sparingly:

While conventional progressions can be comforting, avoid relying on them exclusively. Introduce surprises by deviating from typical chord progressions at strategic points in your composition.

Explore Modal Interchange:

Experiment with modal interchange to introduce surprising harmonies. Borrow chords from related modes to add color and unexpected tonal shifts.

Employ Chromaticism:

Incorporate chromatic elements within your harmonies. Unexpected chromatic chords or passing tones can add a touch of surprise and tension.

Dynamic Harmonic Rhythm:

Vary the harmonic rhythm throughout your composition. Speed up or slow down the rate of chord changes to create moments of unpredictability within the overall structure.

Unexpected Chord Extensions:

Surprise your listeners with chord extensions. Adding seventh, ninth, or eleventh chords where they might not be anticipated can bring richness and intrigue.

Contrast Predictable and Unpredictable Sections:

Structure your composition with sections of predictability followed by sections of surprise. This creates a balanced and dynamic overall progression.

Balance Unison and Harmony:

Combine unison or octave passages with harmonies. Unison can provide a predictable and powerful moment, while harmonies can introduce surprises.

Harmonic Pedals as a Stabilizing Element:

Use harmonic pedals strategically. Sustained tones can act as stabilizing elements amidst surprising harmonic shifts, maintaining a sense of continuity.

Surprising Modulations:

Explore modulations to unexpected keys. Transitioning to a different key can provide a surprising twist, injecting freshness into your harmonic palette.

Create Harmonic Sequences:

Develop harmonic sequences within your composition. Repeating and varying patterns can be both predictable and surprising, depending on how they are employed.

Rhythmic Displacement:

Experiment with rhythmic displacement of harmonic changes. Shifting the timing of chord changes can create unexpected accents and syncopations.

Voice Leading Surprises:

Use unexpected voice leading within chord progressions. Unusual movements between individual voices can add surprising nuances.

Contrasting Dynamics:

Utilize dynamic contrasts to accentuate harmonic surprises. A sudden change in volume or intensity can magnify the impact of unexpected harmonic shifts.

Consider Audience Expectations:

Be aware of the expectations of your target audience. Balancing predictability and surprise should align with the stylistic norms of the genre while pushing creative boundaries.

Evaluate with Objectivity:

Record your composition and listen with fresh ears. Evaluate whether the balance between predictability and surprise enhances the overall emotional and musical impact.

Examples:

Example 1 – Predictable Start, Surprising Bridge:
```

Verse: | CG| AmF|
Bridge: | EGm| CmF|
```

The bridge introduces surprising chords in a section that otherwise follows a predictable pattern.

Example 2 – Chromatic Surprises:
```

Chorus: | CE7| AmAb| GGdim| AmF|
```

Chromatic chords (E7, Ab, Gdim) provide surprising moments within a familiar harmonic context.

Example 3 – Modulation Surprise:
```

Verse: | CG| AmF|
Chorus: | DBm| GEm|
```

The modulation from C major to D major in the chorus introduces a surprising tonal shift.

Balancing predictability and surprise in developing harmonies for guitar composition requires thoughtful experimentation. By strategically incorporating unexpected elements into an otherwise familiar harmonic landscape, you can captivate your audience and keep them engaged from start to finish.

HARMONIZATION TECHNIQUES

Decide on the harmonization techniques you want to employ. Common techniques include parallel harmonies, counterpoint, and thirds/sixths harmonies. Each technique imparts a different feel to the harmonies.

CHOOSING HARMONIZATION TECHNIQUES

Deciding on harmonization techniques is a crucial aspect of crafting a compelling guitar composition. The harmonies you choose can greatly influence the mood, emotion, and overall impact of your music.

Understand the Melodic Structure:
1. Begin by thoroughly understanding the melodic structure of your composition.
2. Identify key phrases, melodic arcs, and points of emotional emphasis.

Consider the Emotional Tone:
1. Reflect on the emotional tone you want to convey through your composition.
2. Different harmonization techniques evoke distinct emotions, so align them with your artistic intent.

Explore Chordal Accompaniment:
1. Decide if you want a chordal accompaniment that follows the melody closely.

2. Experiment with simple triads or more complex extended chords to enhance the harmonic support.

Parallel Harmony:

1. Explore parallel harmony by harmonizing the melody with a consistent interval (e.g., thirds, sixths).
2. This technique often adds a pleasing and consonant quality to the harmonies.

Contrary Motion:

1. Consider using contrary motion, where the harmony moves in the opposite direction of the melody.
2. Contrary motion can create a sense of tension and resolution.

Counterpoint:

1. Delve into counterpoint by crafting independent and complementary lines alongside the melody.
2. Experiment with different contrapuntal techniques, such as imitation and augmentation.

Chromatic Harmonies:

1. Decide if chromatic harmonies can add color and tension to your composition.
2. Use chromaticism selectively for moments of heightened emotion or intrigue.

Modal Harmonies:

1. Explore modal harmonies by incorporating chords from parallel or related modes.

2. Modal harmonies can provide a unique and exotic flavor to your composition.

Pedal Tones:

1. Consider using pedal tones, where a single note is sustained while the harmonies change.
2. Pedal tones add stability and tension, especially when juxtaposed against changing harmonies.

Dynamic Harmonic Progressions:

1. Decide on the dynamic progression of harmonies throughout your composition.
2. Experiment with changing harmonic density and intensity to reflect different sections or emotions.

Experiment with Open Strings:

1. If applicable, experiment with incorporating open strings into your harmonization.
2. Open strings can create resonance and add a lush quality to your harmonies.

Voice Leading:

1. Pay attention to voice leading – the smooth transition of individual voices between chords.
2. Ensure that harmonic changes are logical and contribute to the overall flow.

Harmonic Rhythm:

1. Determine the harmonic rhythm – how frequently the chords change.
2. Adjust the harmonic rhythm to match the pacing and energy of your composition.

Evaluate Guitaristic Playability:

1. Consider the playability of the chosen harmonization techniques on the guitar.
2. Ensure that fingerings are comfortable, and transitions between chords are feasible.

Maintain a Balance:

1. Strike a balance between harmonic complexity and simplicity.
2. Avoid overcrowding the harmonies, allowing space for the melody to shine.

Personal Style and Taste:

1. Infuse your personal style and taste into the harmonization techniques.
2. Consider what resonates with you and aligns with your artistic vision.

Listen Critically:

1. Actively listen to how different harmonization techniques interact with your melody.
2. Make adjustments based on what enhances the overall musical experience.

Deciding on harmonization techniques involves a thoughtful and creative process. By considering the emotional context, experimenting with various harmonic approaches, and staying true to your artistic vision, you can create harmonies that elevate your guitar composition.

Be open to exploration, trust your instincts, and let the harmonization techniques become an integral part of the expressive tapestry of your musical creation.

PARALLEL HARMONIES

Experiment with parallel harmonies, where the harmony moves in the same direction as the melody. This technique often creates a sense of unity and strength.

Experimenting With Parallel Harmonies

Experimenting with parallel harmonies in guitar composition is a creative way to add depth and richness to your music. Parallel harmonies involve accompanying a melody by harmonizing it with another line that moves in the same direction. This technique creates a consonant and pleasing effect.

Select a Melody:
1. Begin with a well-defined melody that you want to harmonize.
2. Identify key notes and phrases within the melody that can be enhanced with harmonies.

Choose a Harmonic Interval:
1. Decide on the harmonic interval you want to use for parallel harmonies.
2. Common intervals include thirds, sixths, and tenths, but feel free to experiment with others.

Create a Parallel Harmony Line:
1. Craft a parallel harmony line that mirrors the melody at the chosen interval.
2. Ensure that the harmonic line flows smoothly and enhances the emotional quality of the melody.

Listen Critically:

1. Record and listen to your composition with parallel harmonies to assess their impact.
2. Make adjustments to achieve the desired emotional and sonic qualities.

Experiment with Thirds:

If you're using thirds for harmonization, create a parallel line where the harmonizing notes are a third above or below the melody.

Example:
```

Melody: C - D - E
Harmony: E - F - G
```

Try Sixths Harmonies:

Explore harmonizing at the interval of sixths, providing a broader and more open sound.

Example:
```

Melody: A - B - C
Harmony: E - F - G
```

Combine Thirds and Sixths:

Experiment with combining thirds and sixths in the same harmonization to add variety.

Example:
```

Melody: G - A - B
Harmony: E - F - G / B - C - D
```

Incorporate Tenths:

For a wider harmonic range, consider incorporating tenths, which are essentially thirds but an octave apart.

Example:
```

Melody: D - E - F
Harmony: B - C - D
```

Explore Octaves:

Experiment with creating parallel harmonies at the octave for a more robust and full-bodied sound.

Example:
```

Melody: G - A - B
Harmony: G - A - B
```

Use Open Strings:

Take advantage of open strings to create resonant parallel harmonies.

Example:
```

Melody: E - F - G
Harmony: B - C - D (with open B and E strings)
```

Consider Articulation Techniques:

Experiment with articulation techniques like legato, staccato, or slides within the parallel harmonies for added expressiveness.

Example:
```

Melody: C - D - E
Harmony: E (slide to F) - F - G
```

Vary Rhythmic Patterns:

Explore different rhythmic patterns in your parallel harmonies to create dynamic interest.

Example:
```

Melody: A - B - C
Harmony: E (sustain) - F (staccato) - G (legato)
```

Blend with Chord Progressions:

Integrate your parallel harmonies with chord progressions that complement the melody.

Example:
```

Chord Progression: Am - G - C
Melody: E - D - C
Harmony: C - B - A
```

Experiment with Different Sections:

Apply parallel harmonies selectively, perhaps emphasizing certain sections of your composition for contrast.

Example:
```

Melody: (Verse) A - B - C / (Chorus) G - A - B
Harmony: (Verse) E - F - G / (Chorus) D - E - F
```

Maintain Balance:

Ensure a balance between the melody and parallel harmonies, avoiding overpowering the main musical line.

Experimenting with parallel harmonies offers a versatile and expressive tool for enhancing your guitar compositions. Whether you opt for thirds, sixths, or other intervals, the key is to listen, refine, and let your creativity guide the harmonic exploration. By incorporating parallel harmonies thoughtfully, you can elevate your melodies and create a captivating musical experience for your audience.

PARALLEL HARMONIES IN MUSIC

Many songs across various genres employ guitar parallel harmonies to create lush and harmonically rich textures.

EXAMPLES IN POPULAR MUSIC

Hotel California by Eagles:

The iconic guitar solo in *Hotel California* features parallel harmonies, contributing to the atmospheric and melodic quality of the solo.

Wish You Were Here by Pink Floyd:

Pink Floyd's *Wish You Were Here* includes parallel harmonies in the acoustic guitar parts, creating a beautiful and emotive sonic landscape.

Sweet Child o' Mine by Guns N' Roses:

The famous guitar intro in *Sweet Child o' Mine* uses parallel harmonies, especially in the ascending arpeggio, adding a melodic and dynamic element.

Hotel California by Eagles:

The outro solo of *Hotel California* is another example where the harmonized guitar parts contribute to the song's overall sound.

More Than a Feeling by Boston:

Boston's *More Than a Feeling* features harmonized guitar lines in the chorus, enhancing the melodic and anthemic quality of the song.

Jessica by The Allman Brothers Band:

The instrumental *Jessica* showcases harmonized guitar lines throughout, creating a joyful and intricate musical tapestry.

Sultans of Swing by Dire Straits:

The guitar solos in *Sultans of Swing* often include parallel harmonies, adding flair and complexity to Mark Knopfler's distinctive playing.

Comfortably Numb by Pink Floyd:

Another Pink Floyd classic, *Comfortably Numb*, features harmonized guitar solos that contribute to the song's epic and emotional atmosphere.

November Rain by Guns N' Roses:

The extended guitar solo in *November Rain* incorporates harmonized sections, showcasing the band's use of layered guitar arrangements.

Blackbird by The Beatles:

Blackbird by The Beatles includes a delicate acoustic guitar part with parallel harmonies, adding a touch of elegance to the song.

Cemetery Gates by Pantera:

Pantera's *Cemetery Gates* features harmonized guitar sections in the solo, combining heavy metal intensity with melodic intricacy.

Little Wing by Jimi Hendrix:

Jimi Hendrix's Little Wing has harmonized guitar parts in the instrumental sections, contributing to the song's dreamy and ethereal quality.

Mr. Crowley by Ozzy Osbourne (Randy Rhoads):

Randy Rhoads showcases harmonized guitar sections in the solo of *Mr. Crowley*, blending neoclassical elements with rock.

Bohemian Rhapsody by Queen:

Queen's *Bohemian Rhapsody* features harmonized guitar lines in various sections, enhancing the song's operatic and theatrical nature.

YYZ by Rush:

The instrumental track YYZ by Rush includes harmonized guitar and bass sections, showcasing the band's progressive and technical prowess.

These examples demonstrate the versatility of parallel harmonies in different musical contexts, from classic rock and metal to acoustic and progressive genres. Each song utilizes harmonies to create a unique sonic fingerprint, contributing to the overall impact and appeal of the music.

CONTRAPUNTAL (COUNTERPOINT) HARMONIES

Explore contrapuntal harmonies, where the harmony moves independently of the melody, creating interwoven lines. This technique adds complexity and interest to the overall texture.

EXPLORING CONTRAPUNTAL HARMONIES

Contrapuntal harmonies, also known as counterpoint, involve the combination of independent and interweaving melodic lines to create a harmonically rich texture. Experimenting with contrapuntal harmonies in guitar composition can elevate your music, adding complexity, depth, and a sense of musical conversation.

Understand Contrapuntal Harmony:

Contrapuntal harmony emphasizes the independence and interaction of melodic lines. Each voice maintains its melodic integrity while harmonizing with others.

Select or Create Melodic Lines:

Begin with two or more distinct melodic lines that can function independently. These could be original compositions or adapted from existing melodies.

Choose Harmonic Progressions:

Decide on a harmonic progression that complements your melodic lines. Ensure that the harmonic changes provide opportunities for interesting contrapuntal interactions.

Experiment with Voice Leading:

Pay close attention to voice leading—how individual voices move from one note to the next. Aim for smooth and logical transitions between chords to maintain a sense of coherence.

CONTRAPUNTAL TECHNIQUES

Explore various contrapuntal techniques, such as **imitation**, **inversion**, and **augmentation**.

Imitation involves one voice repeating or echoing another, while **inversion** and **augmentation** modify the original melodic material.

Use Different Rhythmic Patterns:

Experiment with different rhythmic patterns for each voice to create rhythmic interest. Syncopation, dotted rhythms, and varied note durations can add dynamic contrast.

Balance and Equal Importance:

Ensure that each melodic line receives equal importance. Avoid having one voice overshadow the others. Achieve a balance where each voice contributes to the overall texture.

Layering of Voices:

Consider layering additional voices as your composition progresses. Three or more independent voices can create intricate contrapuntal harmonies.

Explore Canon or Round Structures:

Experiment with canons or rounds where the same melodic material is played by different voices with staggered entrances. This creates a contrapuntal texture with a sense of continuity.

Chromaticism and Dissonance:

Introduce controlled chromaticism and dissonance for added tension and resolution. Use dissonant intervals strategically to enhance the emotional impact of certain moments.

Contrast in Dynamics:

Create contrast in dynamics between different voices to emphasize certain melodic lines. Use dynamic changes to guide the listener's attention.

Combine Contrapuntal and Homophonic Elements:

Integrate contrapuntal harmonies with moments of homophonic texture (harmonized chords). This creates a dynamic interplay between independent voices and unified harmonic statements.

Example 1 – Bach's Two-Part Invention No. 1 in C Major:

Johann Sebastian Bach's Two-Part Invention No. 1 is a classic example of contrapuntal harmony. The two voices engage in a continuous dialogue, showcasing imitative and invertible counterpoint.

Example 2 – "Bouree in E Minor" by Jethro Tull (Adaptation of Bach):

Jethro Tull's adaptation of Bach's "Bouree in E Minor" incorporates contrapuntal harmonies with a rock twist. It features a main melody with additional voices contributing to the overall texture.

Example 3 – "Capricho Arabe" by Francisco Tárrega:

Tárrega's "Capricho Arabe" explores contrapuntal elements within a solo guitar piece. The interplay of voices creates a rich and intricate harmonic landscape.

Recording and Listening:

Record your contrapuntal composition and actively listen to how the voices interact. Identify areas for refinement and ensure clarity in the contrapuntal lines.

Experimenting with contrapuntal harmonies in guitar composition allows you to create intricate and engaging musical conversations between independent voices. By carefully crafting melodic lines, experimenting with voice leading, and exploring various contrapuntal techniques, you can add depth and sophistication to your compositions. As you delve into the world of contrapuntal harmony, keep in mind the balance between complexity and clarity, aiming for a musical experience that captivates the listener.

THIRDS AND SIXTHS HARMONIES

Use thirds and sixths harmonies to create a harmonically pleasing and consonant sound. These intervals often complement the melody without introducing excessive tension.

EXPERIMENTING WITH THIRDS AND SIXTHS

Harmonizing a melody with thirds and sixths adds a beautiful and melodious quality to your guitar compositions. These intervals create a sense of harmony by introducing additional voices that move parallel to the melody. Experimenting with thirds and sixths harmonies allows you to explore various textures and enrich the overall sound of your music.

UNDERSTANDING THIRDS AND SIXTHS

Thirds:

In a harmonic context, a third is an interval that spans three diatonic scale degrees.

Sixths:

Similarly, a sixth is an interval that spans six diatonic scale degrees.

Select a Melody:

Begin with a well-defined melody that you want to harmonize. Identify key notes and phrases within the melody.

EXPERIMENTING WITH THIRDS

Harmonize the melody using thirds by selecting notes that are a third above or below each melody note.

Example:
```
```

Melody: C - D - E
Harmony: E - F - G
```
```

EXPERIMENTING WITH SIXTHS

Harmonize the melody using sixths by selecting notes that are a sixth above or below each melody note.

Example:
```
```

Melody: A - B - C
Harmony: E - F - G
```
```

Combining Thirds and Sixths:
Experiment with combining thirds and sixths in the same harmonization to add variety.
Example:
```
```

Emelody: G - A - B
Harmony: E - F - G / B - C - D
```
```

Incorporate Open Strings:
Take advantage of open strings to create resonant harmonies.

Example:
```

Melody: E - F - G
Harmony: B - C - D (with open B and E strings)
```


Layering Thirds and Sixths:
Experiment with layering different intervals at different points in your composition to create depth.

Example:
```

Melody: D - E - F
Harmony: B - C - D / G - A - B (layering thirds and sixths)
```


Chord Progressions with Harmonies:
Apply thirds and sixths harmonies within chord progressions to create a harmonic bed for your melody.

Example:
```

Chord Progression: Am - G - C
Melody: E - D - C
Harmony: C - B - A (thirds) / G - F - E (sixths)
```

Useful Articulation Techniques:

Experiment with articulation techniques like legato, staccato, or slides within the harmonized lines for added expressiveness.

Example:
```

Melody: C - D - E
Harmony: E (slide to F) - F - G
```

Dynamic Contrasts:

Create dynamic contrasts between the melody and harmonies by adjusting the volume and emphasis of each voice.

Example:
```

Melody: A - B - C
Harmony: E (soft) - F (accented) - G (moderate)
```

Listening and Refining:

Record your composition and actively listen to the interaction between the melody and harmonies.

Make adjustments to achieve a balanced and pleasing blend.

Experiment with Different Genres:

Apply thirds and sixths harmonies in various musical genres, from classical to pop, to discover their versatility.

Explore Contrapuntal Elements:

Incorporate contrapuntal elements by allowing the harmonized lines to move independently and interact melodically.

Example 1 – Blackbird by The Beatles:

The intro to *Blackbird* features a combination of thirds and sixths harmonies, creating a distinctive and evocative sound.

Example 2 – Dust in the Wind by Kansas:

Dust in the Wind incorporates harmonies in thirds and sixths, contributing to the song's acoustic beauty.

Experimenting with thirds and sixths harmonies adds a layer of sophistication to your guitar compositions. These harmonies provide a pleasing and melodious accompaniment to the melody, creating a rich and expressive musical experience. As you explore these intervals, pay attention to the emotional impact they bring to your music, and let your creativity guide you in crafting harmonies that enhance the overall beauty of your guitar compositions.

DISSONANCE

Introduce controlled dissonance for moments of tension and release. Dissonant harmonies, when resolved appropriately, can add emotional depth to your composition.

EXPERIMENTING WITH DISSONANCE

Experimenting with dissonance in guitar composition can add tension, depth, and a unique character to your music. Dissonance, in the context of harmony, refers to the combination of tones that sound unstable or clash with each other. When used strategically, dissonance can be a powerful tool to enhance emotional expression and create engaging compositions.

We explore how to experiment with dissonance to complement the melody in guitar composition in the following sections.

UNDERSTANDING DISSONANCE

Dissonance occurs when intervals or chords create a sense of tension and instability.

It contrasts with **consonance**, which is characterized by stable and harmonious sounds.

Select a Melody:

1. Begin with a melody that you want to enhance with dissonant elements.
2. Identify specific notes or moments where dissonance can be effectively employed.

Dissonant Intervals:

Experiment with dissonant intervals such as minor seconds, tritones, and augmented fourths.

Example:
```

Melody: C - D - E
Dissonance: C (minor second) - D (minor second) - F (minor second)
```

Chromaticism:

Introduce chromaticism to create dissonant passing tones or neighboring tones.

Example:
```

Melody: A - B - C
Dissonance: A♭ (chromatic passing tone) - B♭ (chromatic passing tone) - B (consonant note)
```

Dissonant Chords:

Experiment with dissonant chords, such as diminished or augmented chords, to accompany the melody.

Example:
```

Melody: G - A - B
Dissonant Chord: G7 (includes dissonant tritone interval)
```

Voice Leading in Dissonant Resolutions:

Resolve dissonant intervals through careful voice leading to consonant intervals.

Example:
```

Melody: E - F - G

Dissonance: E (sustained) - F (resolve to G) - G (consonant)
```


Dissonant Articulation:

Experiment with dissonant articulation techniques such as slides, bends, or vibrato to introduce subtle dissonance.

Example:
```

Melody: D - E - F

Dissonant Articulation: E (bend slightly) - F (release bend) - G (consonant)
```


Diatonic Dissonance:

Use diatonic dissonance within the context of a key, exploring tensions that naturally arise from the harmonic series.

Example:
```

Melody: A - B - C

Diatonic Dissonance: B (sus4, diatonic tension) - C (resolve to consonant tonic note)
```

Dissonant Passing Chords:

Introduce passing chords with dissonant qualities to connect different harmonic points.

Example:

```

Chord Progression: Am - E - C
Dissonant Passing Chord: E7 (includes dissonant tritone) between Am and C
```


Experiment with Modal Interchange:

Explore modal interchange to introduce dissonant chords from parallel or related modes.

Example:

```

Melody: D - E - F
Modal Interchange: Em (natural minor) - E7 (includes dissonant D) - Am (resolve)
```


Dissonant Double Stops:

Experiment with dissonant double stops (playing two notes simultaneously) to create a denser harmonic texture.

Example:

```

Melody: G - A - B
Dissonant Double Stops: G and B played simultaneously (dissonant major seventh interval)
```

Dynamic Variation with Dissonance:

Use dynamic variation to emphasize dissonant moments, creating peaks and valleys in tension.

Example:

```

Melody: F - G - A

Dynamic Variation: F (soft) - G (loud, emphasizing dissonant tritone) - A (soft)

```


Listen and Refine:

Record your composition and actively listen to the interplay between dissonant and consonant elements.

Make refinements to balance the tension and resolution.

Example 1 – Eruption by Van Halen:

The guitar solo in *Eruption* incorporates dissonant tapping techniques, creating a dynamic and virtuosic display.

Example 2 – Scar Tissue by Red Hot Chili Peppers:

The opening guitar riff in *Scar Tissue* features a dissonant double stop, contributing to the song's melancholic atmosphere.

Example 3 – Basket Case by Green Day:

The main riff in *Basket Case* includes dissonant power chords, adding an edgy quality to the punk rock sound.

Experimenting with dissonance in guitar composition allows you to infuse your music with tension, drama, and a unique sonic identity. Whether using dissonant intervals, chords, or articulation techniques, the key is to balance moments of tension with resolution. By carefully incorporating dissonance, you can create a dynamic and expressive musical journey that captivates the listener's attention and emotions.

OPEN STRINGS

If possible, incorporate open strings into your harmonies. Open strings can add resonance and a lush quality to the harmonies.

INCORPORATE OPEN STRINGS

Incorporating open strings into your harmonies can add a rich and resonant quality to your guitar compositions. Open strings provide additional color and depth, enhancing the overall texture of your music.

UNDERSTAND OPEN STRING HARMONIES

Open strings are unfretted strings that produce a distinct and resonant sound when played.

Incorporating open strings into your harmonies involves using them in conjunction with fretted notes.

Select a Melody or Chord Progression:
1. Choose a melody or chord progression that allows for the inclusion of open strings.
2. Identify moments where open strings can complement the fretted notes.

Harmonize with Open Strings:
Harmonize the melody by incorporating open strings that resonate harmoniously with the fretted notes.

Example:
```

Melody: E - F - G

Harmony: B (open string) - C (fretted) - D (fretted)
```

Explore Open String Double Stops:

Experiment with double stops, playing two notes simultaneously, where one is an open string.

Example:
```

Melody: A - B - C

Double Stop: A (open string) - B (fretted)
```

Add Open Strings to Chord Voicings:

Include open strings in chord voicings to create lush and resonant chords.

Example:
```

Chord Progression: C - G - Am - F

Open String Voicing: C (open E and G strings) - G (open B string) - Am (open A string) - F (open D string)
```

Create Open String Pedals:

Use open strings as pedal tones, sustaining them while changing the harmony around them.

Example:
```

Chord Progression: D - G - A
Open String Pedal: D (open D string) - G (open G string) - A (open A string)
```


Blend Open and Fretted Notes:

Blend open and fretted notes within a melody to create a seamless transition between different harmonic textures.
Example:
```

Melody: E - F - G
Blend: E (open E string) - F (fretted) - G (fretted)
```


Experiment with Different Open Strings:

Explore the unique resonance and timbre of different open strings to find the most fitting harmonies.
Example:
```

Melody: D - E - F
Harmony: D (open D string) - E (open E string) - F (open B string)
```


Use Open Strings in Arpeggios:

Incorporate open strings into arpeggios, allowing them to ring out while moving through different chord tones.

Example:
```

Chord Progression: C - G - Am - F

Arpeggio: C (open E string) - E (open B string) - G (open D string) - C (open E string)
```


Create Open String Resonance:

Use open strings strategically to create resonance and sustain, adding a warm and ambient quality to your harmonies.

Example:
```

Melody: A - B - C

Resonance: A (open A string) - B (fretted) - C (fretted)
```


Explore Open String Slides:

Experiment with sliding into or out of open strings for a smooth and expressive effect.

Example:
```

Melody: G - A - B

Slide: G (slide into open G string) - A (fretted) - B (fretted)
```

Combine Open String and Barre Chords:

Combine open string voicings with barre chords to create a blend of open resonance and fretted complexity.

Example:

```

Chord Progression: E - B - A
Voicing: E (open E string) - B (barre chord) - A (open A string)

```

Listen and Refine:

Record your composition and actively listen to how the open strings enhance the harmonic quality.

Adjust the balance between open and fretted notes for optimal resonance.

Example 1 – Dust in the Wind by Kansas:

The iconic fingerpicking pattern in *Dust in the Wind* incorporates open strings, creating a delicate and melodic texture.

Example 2 – Blackbird by The Beatles:

Blackbird utilizes open strings to complement the intricate fingerstyle picking, contributing to the song's distinctive sound.

Example 3 – Angie by The Rolling Stones:

Angie features open string arpeggios that add a shimmering quality to the melancholic melody.

Incorporating open strings into your guitar harmonies opens up a world of sonic possibilities. The resonance and sustain of open strings can provide a beautiful backdrop to your melodies and chords. Experiment with different approaches, be it double stops, chord voicings, or pedal tones, and let the natural resonance of open strings enhance the depth and expressiveness of your guitar compositions.

INVERSIONS

Explore chord inversions for harmonies. Inverting chords can create smooth voice leading and contribute to a more fluid and connected harmonic progression.

EXPLORING CHORD INVERSIONS

Exploring chord inversions in guitar composition can significantly enhance the harmonic richness and flow of your music. Chord inversions involve rearranging the order of a chord's notes while maintaining the same pitches. By incorporating inversions, you can create smoother voice leading, add variety to your harmonic progressions, and achieve a more sophisticated sound.

UNDERSTANDING CHORD INVERSIONS

A chord inversion involves changing the order of the chord tones while keeping the same notes.

Root position:
The original order of the chord tones.

First inversion:
The root is moved to the top of the chord.

Second inversion:
The third is moved to the top.

SELECT A CHORD PROGRESSION

Choose a chord progression from your composition that can benefit from smoother voice leading or a different harmonic texture.

Explore Root Position:
Begin with the chords in root position to establish the foundation.
Example:
```

Chord Progression: C - G - Am - F
Root Position: C - G - Am - F
```

Move to First Inversion:
Experiment with moving the root of each chord to the top to create first inversions.
Example:
```

First Inversion: E - G - C - F
```

Experiment with Second Inversion:
Move the third of each chord to the top to create second inversions.
Example:
```

Second Inversion: G - C - E - F
```

Smooth Voice Leading:

Use inversions to achieve smoother voice leading between chords, minimizing the distance between consecutive chords.

Example:
```

Root Position: C - E - G
First Inversion: E - G - C (smooth voice leading to Am)
```

Invert Partial Chords:

Consider inverting only a portion of a chord, especially if certain tones remain static.

Example:
```

Chord: C - E - G
Partial Inversion: C - G - E (keeping the root static)
```

Create Bass Movement:

Utilize inversions to create interesting bass movements within your chord progressions.

Example:
```

Root Position: C - G - Am - F
Bass Movement in Inversions: C - G/B - Am/C - F
```

Combine Inversions and Open Strings:

Combine chord inversions with open strings to add resonance and depth to your harmonies.

Example:

```

Chord Progression: C - G - Am - F
Inversions with Open Strings: C/G - G/B - Am - F (using open strings for G/B and F)
```

Useful Inversions for Guitar:

For major chords, first inversion often works well. For minor chords, consider both first and second inversions.

Example:

```

Major Chord (C): C - E - G
First Inversion: E - G - C
Minor Chord (Am): A - C - E
First Inversion: C - E - A
Second Inversion: E - A - C
```

Chord Progression with Inversions:

Apply inversions to a chord progression to witness the harmonic variety they bring.

Example:
```

Chord Progression: D - Bm - G - A
Root Position: D - Bm - G - A
First Inversion: F - Bm - G - E
Second Inversion: A - F - G - E
```

Create Movement with Inversions:

Use inversions to create ascending or descending movement within your harmonic progressions.
Example:
```

Chord Progression: C - Am - F - G
Root Position Movement: C - Am - F - G
Inversion Movement: C - Am - F/A - G/B
```

Melody Harmonization with Inversions:

Harmonize a melody using inversions to create varied and interesting chord accompaniments.
Example:
```

Melody: C - D - E
Harmonization: C - E/G - Am - F (using inversions to complement the melody)
```

Listen and Refine:

Record your chord progressions with inversions and actively listen to the nuanced harmonic changes.

Refine the inversions to achieve the desired emotional impact and fluidity.

Example 1 – Yesterday by The Beatles:

The chord progression in *Yesterday* features effective use of inversions, contributing to the song's melancholic atmosphere.

Example 2 – Fields of Gold by Sting:

Fields of Gold utilizes inversions to create a smooth and flowing chord progression that complements the melodic line.

Example 3 – Stairway to Heaven by Led Zeppelin:

The iconic intro of *Stairway to Heaven* incorporates inversions, creating a dynamic and evolving harmonic landscape.

Exploring chord inversions for harmonies in guitar composition opens up a realm of possibilities for creating nuanced and sophisticated musical expressions. Whether aiming for smoother voice leading, creating interesting bass movements, or enhancing the overall harmonic texture, inversions provide a valuable tool in your compositional arsenal. Experiment with different chord progressions and inversions to discover the unique flavors they bring to your guitar compositions.

ARPEGGIOS

Harmonize your melody with arpeggios derived from the underlying chords. Arpeggiated harmonies can create a flowing and intricate accompaniment.

HARMONIZING WITH ARPEGGIOS

Harmonizing your melody with arpeggios derived from the underlying chords is a captivating technique that adds depth and dimension to your guitar composition. Arpeggios allow you to outline the chord tones in a melodic and flowing manner, creating a harmonically rich accompaniment to your melody.

Select a Melody:
Begin with a melody that you want to harmonize. Identify the key notes and phrases within the melody.

Identify Underlying Chords:
Determine the underlying chords that accompany your melody. This involves understanding the harmonic progression supporting the melody.

Derive Arpeggios:
Extract arpeggios from the underlying chords. An arpeggio is a broken chord where the notes are played in a sequence rather than simultaneously.

Coordinate Arpeggios with Melody:
Harmonize your melody by integrating the arpeggios with the melodic line. Assign arpeggios to coincide with specific melody notes.

Explore Different Arpeggio Patterns:

Experiment with various arpeggio patterns, such as ascending, descending, or mixed patterns, to add variety and interest.

Example:
```

Melody: C - D - E
Arpeggio Pattern 1: C E G (ascending)
Arpeggio Pattern 2: G E C (descending)
```


Combine Chords and Arpeggios:

Combine full chords with arpeggios to create a lush and dynamic harmonic background for your melody.

Example:
```

Chord: C - E - G
Arpeggio: C E G (arpeggiated)
```


Arpeggio Inversions:

Experiment with arpeggio inversions to achieve smooth voice leading between different chords.

Example:
```

Chord: C - E - G
Inverted Arpeggio: E G C
```

Use of Open Strings:

Incorporate open strings within arpeggios for added resonance and a unique sound.

Example:
```
```

Chord: Am - C - G

Arpeggio with Open Strings: A E C (Am) - E G C (C) - G D B (G)
```
```


Apply Dynamics:

Use dynamics to emphasize certain notes within the arpeggios, creating a dynamic and expressive performance.

Example:
```
```

Arpeggio: C E G (soft) - E G C (loud) - G C E (soft)
```
```


Syncopated Arpeggios:

Experiment with syncopated rhythms within the arpeggios to add rhythmic interest.

Example:
```
```

Arpeggio: C E G (quarter notes) - E G C (eighth notes) - G C E (quarter notes)
```
```


Harmonize Diatonic Progressions:

Harmonize diatonic progressions with arpeggios for a classic and pleasing sound.

Arpeggios
Example:
```

Melody: D - E - F - G - A - B
Diatonic Harmonization: D F A (D) - E G B (E minor) - F A C (F minor) - G B D (G) - A C E (A) - B D F (B minor)
```


Use of Arpeggio Runs:

Incorporate arpeggio runs, where arpeggios flow consecutively, creating a cascading effect.
Example:
```

Chord Progression: Am - G - F - C
Arpeggio Runs: A C E (Am) - G B D (G) - F A C (F) - C E G (C)
```


Add Color Tones:

Introduce color tones or extensions within the arpeggios for added richness.
Example:
```

Chord: Cmaj7 – E7 – Am
Arpeggio with Color Tones: C E G B (Cmaj7) - E G B D (E7) - A C E G (Am)
```


Create Arpeggio Patterns for Modal Harmony:

Experiment with arpeggio patterns that reflect modal harmonies for a more modal or exotic sound.

Example:
```

Chord Progression: Dm - G - C
Modal Arpeggio Patterns: D F A (D Dorian) - G B D
(G Mixolydian) - C E G (C Ionian)
```

Record and Evaluate:
Record your harmonized melody with arpeggios and actively listen to the interplay between the melodic line and harmonic accompaniment.

Refine and adjust as needed to achieve the desired emotional impact.

Example 1 – Classical Gas by Mason Williams:
The iconic fingerstyle piece *Classical Gas* harmonizes the melody with intricate arpeggios, creating a complex and beautiful texture.

Example 2 – Tears in Heaven by Eric Clapton:
The acoustic ballad *Tears in Heaven* utilizes arpeggios to harmonize the delicate and heartfelt melody.

Example 3 – Hotel California by Eagles:
The outro of *Hotel California* features harmonized arpeggios, contributing to the song's signature sound.

Harmonizing your melody with arpeggios is a powerful technique that can elevate the expressiveness of your guitar composition.

Arpeggios

By carefully selecting arpeggio patterns, incorporating inversions, and experimenting with rhythmic elements, you can create a captivating interplay between the melodic and harmonic aspects of your music. Whether aiming for a classical, folk, or contemporary sound, the use of arpeggios provides a versatile and expressive tool for enriching your guitar compositions.

HARMONY AND DIFFERENT REGISTERS

Explore harmonies in different registers on the guitar. Harmonizing in higher or lower octaves can add variation and depth to the overall sound.

UTILIZING DIFFERENT REGISTERS

Exploring harmonies in different registers on the guitar opens up a world of sonic possibilities, allowing you to create rich, layered textures and enhance the depth of your composition. By utilizing various registers, you can achieve a balanced and well-rounded harmonic palette.

UNDERSTAND GUITAR REGISTERS

The guitar has multiple registers, including low, mid, and high. Each register contributes a unique timbre to the overall sound.

Select a Chord Progression:

Choose a chord progression from your composition that you want to explore in different registers.

Low Register Harmonies:

Experiment with playing chord progressions in the lower register for a warm and resonant foundation.

Example:
```

Chord Progression: C - G - Am - F
Low Register Harmonies: (Low voicings)
C: x 3 2 0 1 0
G: 3 2 0 0 0 3
Am: x 0 2 2 1 0
F: 1 3 3 2 1 1
```

Mid Register Harmonies:

Transition to the mid register for a balanced and versatile sound, suitable for both rhythm and melody.

Example:
```

Chord Progression: C - G - Am - F
Mid Register Harmonies: (Mid voicings)
C: x 3 2 0 1 0
G: 3 2 0 0 0 3
Am: 5 7 7 5 5 5
F: 1 3 3 2 1 1
```

High Register Harmonies:

Explore the high register for a brighter and more intricate sound, suitable for adding sparkle and emphasis.

Example:

```

Chord Progression: C - G - Am - F
High Register Harmonies: (High voicings)
C: 8 10 9 0 0 0
G: 10 9 7 0 0 0
Am: 12 14 14 12 13 12
F: 13 15 15 14 13 13

```

Arpeggios Across Registers:

Play arpeggios across different registers to create movement and dynamics within your chord progressions.

Example:

```

Chord Progression: C - G - Am - F
Arpeggios Across Registers: (Arpeggiated patterns)
C: (Low register arpeggio)
G: (Mid register arpeggio)
Am: (High register arpeggio)
F: (Mid register arpeggio)

```

Voice Leading Between Registers:

Experiment with smooth voice leading between registers to create seamless transitions.

Example:
```

Chord Progression: C - G - Am - F
Voice Leading: (Smooth transitions between low, mid, and high registers)
```


Octave Doubling:

Double certain chord tones or the entire chord in a higher or lower octave to add richness.

Example:
```

Chord Progression: C - G - Am - F
Octave Doubling: (Higher octave doubling for emphasis)
C: x 3 2 0 1 8
G: 3 2 0 0 0 10
Am: 5 7 7 5 5 12
F: 1 3 3 2 1 13
```


Chord Inversions:

Incorporate chord inversions to create harmonic interest and distribute chord tones across different registers.

Example:
```

Chord Progression: C - G - Am - F
Chord Inversions: (Inverted voicings in different registers)
```


Use of Open Strings:

Integrate open strings within different registers to enhance resonance and create a full-bodied sound.

Example:
```

Chord Progression: C - G - Am - F
Open String Voicings: (Combining open strings with chords in various registers)
```


Dynamic Contrast Between Registers:

Explore dynamic contrast by playing certain sections in a specific register to emphasize emotional impact.

Example:
```

Chord Progression: C - G - Am - F
Dynamics: (Playing the chorus in a higher register for intensity)
```

Contrast in Texture:

Utilize different registers to create contrast in texture, especially between verses and choruses.

Example:
```

Chord Progression: C - G - Am - F
Texture Contrast: (Verse in mid register, Chorus in high register)
```


Harmonizing Melody Across Registers:

Harmonize your melody across different registers using chord tones or arpeggios.

Example:
```

Melody: C - D - E
Harmonization Across Registers: (Harmonizing the melody in low, mid, and high registers)
```


Recording and Adjusting:

Record your exploration of harmonies in different registers and actively listen to the overall balance and impact.

Adjust the voicings and register choices based on the desired emotional expression.

Example 1 – Hotel California by Eagles:

The iconic introduction of *Hotel California* explores harmonies in different registers, contributing to its atmospheric sound.

Example 2 – Blackbird by The Beatles:

Blackbird features intricate harmonies in the mid to high registers, creating a delicate and melodic texture.

Example 3 – Dust in the Wind by Kansas:

The fingerpicking pattern in *Dust in the Wind* utilizes harmonies in various registers, contributing to its timeless quality.

Exploring harmonies in different registers on the guitar allows you to paint with a broad sonic palette. Whether focusing on the warmth of the low register, the versatility of the mid register, or the sparkle of the high register, each contributes to the overall texture of your composition. By strategically incorporating different registers, you can enhance the expressiveness and depth of your guitar music, creating a captivating listening experience.

HARMONIC LAYERS

Build harmonic layers by adding more than one harmony to your melody. This can create a lush and textured harmonic backdrop.

Building Harmonic Layers

Building harmonic layers by adding more than one harmony to your melody is a powerful technique that can elevate your guitar composition, creating a lush and intricate soundscape. This approach involves incorporating multiple harmonies that complement the melody, resulting in a rich tapestry of chords and textures.

Select a Melody:
Begin with a melody that you want to harmonize. Identify the key notes and phrases within the melody.

Identify Underlying Chords:
Determine the underlying chords that accompany your melody. Understand the harmonic progression supporting the melody.

Add a Simple Harmony:
Start by adding a basic harmony to the melody. This can be a third, a fifth, or a complementary chord tone.
Example:
```

Melody: C - D - E
Harmony (Third): E - F - G
```

Explore Diatonic Harmonies:

Experiment with harmonies derived from the diatonic scale to maintain a natural and pleasing sound.

Example:
```

Melody: A - B - C
Diatonic Harmonies: A - Bm - C
```

Add a Second Harmony:

Introduce a second harmony, creating a more layered effect. Ensure the second harmony complements both the melody and the first harmony.

Example:
```

Melody: G - A - B
First Harmony: B - C - D
Second Harmony: D - E - F
```

Experiment with Intervalic Harmonies:

Utilize different intervals such as thirds, sixths, and tenths to create interesting and varied harmonic layers.

Example:
```

Melody: E - F - G
Third Harmony: G - A - B
Sixth Harmony: C - D - E
```

Add Chordal Layers:

Integrate full chords that harmonize with the melody. Experiment with voicings and inversions.

Example:
```

Melody: C - D - E
Chordal Layers: C - Dm - Em
```


Use of Open Strings:

Incorporate open strings within your harmonies to add resonance and a unique quality to the layers.

Example:
```

Melody: G - A - B
Harmonic Layers with Open Strings: G - Am - Bm
```


Create Contrapuntal Lines:

Develop harmonies that move independently, creating a contrapuntal texture that adds complexity.

Example:
```

Melody: F - G - A
Contrapuntal Harmonies: F - G - Am (bass moves independently)
```


Add Suspensions and Resolutions:

Introduce suspended chords and resolve them to create tension and release within the harmonic layers.

Example:

```

Melody: D - E - F

Harmonic Layers with Suspensions: D - Esus4 - E
```

Explore Extended Chords:

Incorporate extended chords (7th, 9th, 11th) to add sophistication to your harmonic layers.

Example:

```

Melody: A - B - C

Extended Harmonies: A7 - Bm9 - Cmaj11
```

Voice Leading Between Layers:

Pay attention to smooth voice leading between the different harmonic layers for a seamless transition.

Example:

```

Melody: E - F - G

Harmonic Layers Voice Leading: E - Fm - G
```

Build Climaxes with Layers:

Use additional harmonic layers to build towards climactic points in your composition, enhancing emotional intensity.

Example:
```

Melody Climax: G - A - B
Additional Layers: Em - G - A - Bm
```

Contrast Dynamics Between Layers:

Experiment with dynamic contrasts between different layers to create a more dynamic and expressive performance.
Example:
```

Melody: D - E - F
Dynamic Contrasts: D - Dm (soft) - E - Em (soft) - F - Fm (loud)
```

Use of Harmonic Rhythm:

Vary the harmonic rhythm (rate at which chords change) between layers to add interest and complexity.
Example:
```

Melody: C - D - E
Harmonic Rhythm Variation: C - G (held) - Am - F (held) - C
```

Record and Evaluate:

Record your composition with the added harmonic layers and actively listen to the overall harmonic progression and the interplay between layers. Adjust and refine the layers based on the desired emotional impact.

Example 1 – While My Guitar Gently Weeps by The Beatles:

The harmonic layers in the guitar accompaniment contribute to the depth and emotion of the melody.

Example 2 – Scarborough Fair/Canticle by Simon & Garfunkel:

This classic folk song features intricate harmonic layers that enhance the haunting beauty of the melody.

Example 3 – Landslide by Fleetwood Mac:

Landslide employs harmonic layers that build gradually, contributing to the emotional intensity of the composition.

Building harmonic layers by adding more than one harmony to your melody is a versatile and expressive technique for guitar composition. Whether using simple intervals, extended chords, or contrapuntal lines, these layers can create a captivating and sophisticated musical experience. Experiment with different combinations, be attentive to voice leading, and let the harmonic layers enhance the emotional depth of your guitar compositions.

HARMONY DENSITY

Vary the density of your harmonies throughout the composition. Use denser harmonies in climactic moments and more sparse harmonies during subdued sections.

VARYING HARMONIC DENSITY

Varying the density of harmonies throughout your guitar composition is a nuanced approach that adds dynamism and emotional depth to your music. By strategically manipulating the thickness and sparsity of harmonies, you can create moments of tension, release, and emphasis, contributing to the overall narrative of your composition.

Read on about how and why to vary the density of harmonies.

UNDERSTAND HARMONIC DENSITY

Harmonic density refers to the thickness or richness of the harmonic texture at any given moment in your composition.

Determine Musical Context:

Consider the emotional and thematic context of different sections in your composition. Decide where you want moments of intensity, relaxation, or transition.

Why Vary Harmonic Density:

Expressive Dynamics: Varying density creates expressive dynamics, guiding the listener through a sonic journey with moments of tension and resolution.

Highlight Melodic Elements:

Sparse harmonies can highlight individual melodic lines, enhancing their prominence and emotional impact.

Create Contrast:

Alternating between dense and sparse harmonies creates contrast, making your composition more engaging and captivating.

Start with a Simple Melody:

Begin with a simple melody and build harmonies gradually, allowing density to evolve in accordance with the melodic development.

Example:

```
Simple Melody: C - D - E
Initial Harmony: C - G - Am
Gradual Density Increase: Cmaj7 - G - Am9
```

Sparse Harmonies for Emphasis:

Use sparse harmonies during pivotal moments in your composition to emphasize specific phrases or transitions.

Example:
```

Melodic Climax: G - A - B
Sparse Harmonies: G - (Silence) - A - B
```

Dense Harmonies for Intensity:

Increase harmonic density in sections where you want to build intensity or create a climactic moment.
Example:
```

Building Intensity: C - G - Am - F (Normal Density)
Intense Climax: Cmaj7 - G9 - Am7 - Fadd9 (Increased Density)
```

Contrast Within Sections:

Within a section, vary the harmonic density to maintain interest and avoid monotony.
Example:
```

Verse: G - C - D (Sparse)
Chorus: Gmaj7 - Cadd9 - D/F (Dense)
```

Layering Harmonies Gradually:

Gradually layer harmonies throughout a section, starting with simplicity and adding complexity.

Example:
```

Intro: Em - D - C (Sparse)
Development: Em - D/F - Gadd9 - Cadd9 (Increasing Density)
```

Sparse Open Chords vs. Dense Voicings:
Utilize open chords for a sparse sound and move to denser voicings to create a sense of progression.
Example:
```

Sparse: C - G - Am (Open Chords)
Dense: Cmaj7 - G9 - Am7 (Barre Chords)
```

Alternate Between Single Notes and Chords:
Create variety by alternating between single notes and full chords, adjusting harmonic density accordingly.
Example:
```

Melody: C - D - E (Single Notes)
Dense Harmony: Cmaj7 - G - Am9 (Chords)
```

Density Variations in Sections:
Plan density variations between sections of your composition to give each part a distinctive character.

Example:
```

Verse: A - D - E (Sparse)
Bridge: Aadd9 - D/F - Esus4 (Dense)
```


Dynamic Swells with Density:

Increase harmonic density gradually to create dynamic swells, building tension before resolving.

Example:
```

Building Tension: C - G - Am (Low Density)
Resolving: Cmaj7 - Gadd9 - Am9 (Increased Density)
```


Sparse Harmonies for Melancholy Moments:

Sparse harmonies can evoke a sense of melancholy or introspection, especially in slower tempos.

Example:
```

Melancholic Section: Dm - G - Em (Sparse)
```


Gradual Density Decrease for Outro:

Gradually decrease harmonic density in an outro to create a sense of conclusion and resolution.

Example:

```

Climax: A - B - C (Dense)
Outro: A - Bm7 - Cmaj7 (Gradual Density Decrease)

```

Record and Refine:

Record your composition, paying attention to the ebb and flow of harmonic density. Refine as needed to achieve the desired emotional impact.

Example 1 – Blackbird by The Beatles:

The iconic fingerstyle piece *Blackbird* employs varying harmonic density to create moments of delicacy and intensity.

Example 2 – Wish You Were Here by Pink Floyd:

In the song's intro, sparse harmonies gradually build in density, creating a climactic moment before returning to simplicity.

Example 3 – Tears in Heaven by Eric Clapton:

The composition features sections with both sparse and dense harmonies, contributing to the emotional ebb and flow.

Varying the density of harmonies throughout your guitar composition is a sophisticated technique that enhances expressiveness and engages the listener.

By strategically choosing when to introduce sparse or dense harmonies, you can shape the emotional landscape of your music, creating a captivating and dynamic listening experience. Experiment with these concepts to find the harmonic density variations that best suit the narrative of your composition.

HARMONY AND MELODIC CONTOUR

Adapt your harmonies to the contour and phrasing of the melody. Align the harmonic changes with important melodic accents and shape the harmonies accordingly.

ADAPTING HARMONIES TO MELODIC CONTOUR

Adapting your harmonies to the contour and phrasing of the melody is a crucial aspect of creating a harmonically rich and emotionally resonant guitar composition. By aligning harmonies with the natural flow and nuances of the melody, you can enhance the expressiveness and coherence of your music.

Analyze Melodic Contour:

Examine the rise and fall, peaks, and valleys of the melody. Understand its contour and overall shape.

Identify Phrasing Patterns:

Recognize the phrasing patterns within the melody, including where phrases start and end, as well as any subtle nuances.

Choose Harmonic Colors:

Select harmonies that complement the emotional quality of the melody. Consider major, minor, suspended, or extended chords based on the mood.

Align Harmonies with Melodic Peaks:

Place harmonies at points where the melody reaches high points, emphasizing and supporting climactic moments.

Example:

```
```

Melody: C - E - G - A - G - F - D

Harmonies: C - Em - G - Am - G - F - Dm

```
```

Adapt Harmonies to Melodic Descents:

Utilize harmonies that mirror the descent of the melody, creating a seamless and connected musical journey.

Example:

```
```

Melody: G - F - E - D - C

Harmonies: G - Fmaj7 - Em - Dm - C

```
```

Harmonic Punctuation at Phrasing Endings:

Introduce harmonic punctuation, such as cadences or extended chords, at the end of melodic phrases to provide closure.

Example:

```
```

Melody: A - B - G - F - E

Harmonies: A - Bm - Gmaj7 - Fm - E

```
```

Explore Chord Inversions:

Experiment with chord inversions to align with melodic peaks or descents, allowing for smooth voice leading.

Example:
```

Melody: E - F - G - A - G - F - E
Harmonies: E - Fm/A - G - Am - G - Fm - E
```


Use Suspending Harmonies for Suspense:

Introduce sus4 or sus2 chords to create tension and suspense at points where the melody holds or pauses.

Example:
```

Melody Pause: C - (Hold) - D
Harmonies: Csus4 - (Hold) - D
```


Add Harmonic Embellishments:

Include embellishments, such as passing chords or added tones, to enhance melodic phrases and add harmonic interest.

Example:
```

Melody: D - E - F - G
Harmonies with Embellishments: D - E7sus4 - Fm11 - G6
```

Align Harmonies with Melodic Articulation:

Match the articulation of the harmonies with the melodic phrasing, emphasizing staccato or legato qualities.

Example:
```

Melody: A (Staccato) - B (Legato) - G (Staccato)
Harmonies: A (Staccato) - Bm9 (Legato) - G (Staccato)
```


Vary Harmonic Density with Melodic Density:

Adjust the density of harmonies based on the density of the melody. Sparse melodies may be complemented by simpler harmonies.

Example:
```

Sparse Melody: C - (Pause) - D
Harmonies: C - (Silence) - D
```


Align Harmonies with Melodic Articulation:

Match the articulation of the harmonies with the melodic phrasing, emphasizing staccato or legato qualities.

Example:
```

Melody: A (Staccato) - B (Legato) - G (Staccato)
Harmonies: A (Staccato) - Bm9 (Legato) - G (Staccato)
```

Explore Modal Harmonies:

Adapt harmonies to modal characteristics when the melody suggests a modal tonality, providing a unique flavor.

Example:
```

Melody: D - E - F - G - A
Harmonies: Dmaj7 - E7 - Fm - Gmaj9 - A
```


Harmonic Rhythm Variation:

Vary the harmonic rhythm to align with melodic phrasing, creating a more dynamic and organic relationship.

Example:
```

Melody: C - D - E - D
Harmonic Rhythm: C - D7 - Em - D9
```


Record and Evaluate:

Record your adaptation of harmonies to the melody and actively listen for the synergy between the two elements.

Adjust and refine as needed to enhance the musicality.

Example 1 – Yesterday by The Beatles:

The harmonies in *Yesterday* follow the contour of the melancholic melody, enhancing its emotional impact.

Example 2 – Wonderful Tonight by Eric Clapton:

Harmonies in this song align with the phrasing of the tender melody, creating a cohesive and expressive musical narrative.

Example 3 – Autumn Leaves (Instrumental Version):

In instrumental versions of *Autumn Leaves*, harmonies adapt to the contour and phrasing of the melody, creating a dynamic interplay.

Adapting your harmonies to the contour and phrasing of the melody is a nuanced art that elevates the musicality of your guitar composition. By carefully aligning harmonies with the natural flow and expressive nuances of the melody, you create a seamless and compelling musical narrative. Experiment with these techniques, allowing your harmonies to breathe life into the melody and enhance the emotional resonance of your guitar compositions.

MELODIC INDEPENDENCE

Ensure that your harmonies do not overpower the melody. Maintain melodic independence, allowing the melody to shine while the harmonies provide support and enhancement.

BALANCING HARMONY AND MELODY

Ensuring that your harmonies do not overpower the melody is crucial in maintaining a balanced and engaging guitar composition. While harmonies enhance the overall musical experience, they should complement the melody rather than overshadow it.

Melody Clarity:

Keep the melody clear and prominent. It should be easily distinguishable, serving as the focal point of your composition.

Dynamic Balance:

Pay attention to the dynamics of both the melody and harmonies. Ensure that the melody has moments of emphasis and that the harmonies don't consistently overshadow it.

Volume Levels:

Adjust the volume levels of your guitar playing, emphasizing the melody while allowing the harmonies to provide a supportive backdrop. Use dynamics to create contrast.

Harmonic Voicings:

Choose harmonic voicings that complement the melody rather than competing with it. Opt for voicings that leave space for the melody to shine.

Avoiding Overly Complex Harmonies:

Be mindful of using overly complex harmonies that may distract from the simplicity and beauty of the melody. Harmonies should enhance, not overwhelm.

Selective Ornamentation:

If adding ornamentation or embellishments to the harmonies, be selective. Ensure that these additions do not obscure the clarity of the melody.

Strategic Use of Dynamics:

Employ dynamics effectively to highlight the melody during crucial moments. Soften harmonies during melodic peaks to prevent overpowering.

Equal Articulation:

Maintain equal articulation between the melody and harmonies. Avoid overly legato or staccato harmonies that may disrupt the flow of the melody.

Frequency Spectrum:

Consider the frequency spectrum. If your harmonies occupy a similar range as the melody, they might clash. Choose harmonic voicings that complement the melodic range.

Experiment with Register:

Explore different registers for harmonies. Placing harmonies in a different octave or range can prevent them from competing with the melody.

Simplifying Harmonies:

During intricate melodic passages, simplify harmonies to avoid overcrowding the musical landscape. Gradually reintroduce complexity when the melody allows.

Strategic Rests:

Introduce brief rests within the harmonies to create space for the melody. Silence can be as powerful as sound in emphasizing the importance of the melody.

Avoiding Unnecessary Ornamentation:

While ornamentation can add flair, be cautious not to overwhelm the melody with excessive embellishments in the harmonies. Ensure that ornamentation serves the musical narrative.

Listening Balance:

Actively listen to your composition. If the harmonies overpower the melody during playback, consider adjustments to maintain a harmonious balance.

Recording and Adjusting:

Record your composition and critically evaluate the balance between melody and harmonies. Make adjustments to achieve the desired equilibrium.

Collaborative Playing:

If playing with other musicians, communicate and collaborate to ensure everyone is aware of the balance needed between melody and harmonies.

Example – Tears in Heaven by Eric Clapton:

The harmonies in this song provide a delicate backdrop, allowing the heartfelt melody to take center stage, creating a perfect balance.

Example – Blackbird by The Beatles:

In *Blackbird*, the harmonies gracefully support the intricate picking of the melody without overshadowing it, showcasing a harmonious coexistence.

Example – Classical Gas by Mason Williams:

This instrumental piece demonstrates a careful balance between the intricate harmonies and the melody, showcasing each element with clarity.

Achieving the right balance between melody and harmonies in your guitar composition is essential for creating a captivating and cohesive musical experience. By implementing these techniques, you can ensure that your harmonies enhance the melody rather than overpower it, allowing the beauty of both elements to shine through in harmony.

MODAL INTERCHANGE

Explore modal interchange by incorporating chords from related modes. This can introduce unexpected harmonies that add color and interest to your composition.

EXPERIMENTING WITH MODAL INTERCHANGE

Experimenting with modal interchange for harmonies in guitar composition is a fascinating way to add color and unexpected twists to your music. Modal interchange involves borrowing chords or harmonic elements from a parallel or related key, introducing fresh and unique flavors to your harmonies.

Understand Modal Interchange:

Modal interchange involves borrowing chords or notes from a parallel or related mode while maintaining the tonic (root) note of the original key.

Identify Modal Possibilities:

Explore modes related to your composition's key. Common choices include borrowing chords from the parallel major or minor, as well as modes like Dorian, Phrygian, or Mixolydian.

Experiment with Major and Minor Borrowing:

For a major key composition, experiment with borrowing chords from its parallel minor, and vice versa. This introduces unexpected tonal colors.

Example:
```

Original: C Major - F - G
Borrowed from C Minor: Cm - F - G
```

Create Tonal Contrast:

Use modal interchange to create tonal contrast within a section. This can add emotional depth and interest to your composition.
Example:
```

Original: A Minor - Dm - E
Borrowed from A Major: Am - D - E
```

Modal Interchange in a Minor Key:

In a minor key, experiment with borrowing chords from the parallel major, introducing a brighter sound.
Example:
```

Original: D Minor - G - Am
Borrowed from D Major: D - G - A
```

Dorian and Mixolydian Borrowing:

Explore borrowing chords from modes like Dorian or Mixolydian to introduce unique harmonic qualities.

Example:
```

Original: G Major - C - D
Borrowed from G Mixolydian: G - C - D7
```

Chromatic Mediant Borrowing:

Experiment with borrowing chords whose roots are a third apart, creating a chromatic mediant relationship. This can add a touch of tension.

Example:
```

Original: E Major - A - B
Chromatic Mediant Borrowing: E - Ab - B
```

Phrygian Borrowing for Intensity:

Borrow chords from the parallel Phrygian mode to add intensity and a slightly exotic feel.

Example:
```

Original: F Major - Bb - C
Borrowed from F Phrygian: Fm - Bb - C
```

Secondary Dominants:

Introduce secondary dominant chords by borrowing from related keys, enhancing the harmonic progression.

Example:
```

Original: C Major - F - G
Secondary Dominant Borrowing: C - D7 - G
```

Experimenting with Modal Borrowing Sequences:

Create harmonic sequences by experimenting with modal interchange. This can lead to interesting chord progressions.

Example:
```

Original: E Minor - Am - B7
Modal Borrowing Sequence: E - A - Cm - F7 - B7
```

Borrowing Diminished or Augmented Chords:

Experiment with borrowing diminished or augmented chords to add tension and unique harmonic color.

Example:
```

Original: D Major - G - A
Diminished Chord Borrowing: D - Gdim - A
```

Experimenting with Harmonic Minor Borrowing:

Borrow chords from the harmonic minor scale for a touch of exoticism and heightened tension.

Example:
```

Original: A Minor - Dm - E
Harmonic Minor Borrowing: Am - Dm - E7
```

Modal Interchange in Fingerstyle Progressions:

Apply modal interchange concepts to fingerstyle guitar progressions, carefully choosing voicings that suit the mood.

Example:
```

Original Fingerstyle: C - G/B - Am
Modal Interchange Fingerstyle: C - G - A7/C
```

Smooth Voice Leading with Borrowed Chords:

Ensure smooth voice leading when incorporating borrowed chords. This maintains coherence and musical flow.

Example:
```

Original: G Major - C - D
Smooth Voice Leading with Borrowing: G - E7 - Am - D
```

Record and Evaluate:

Record your experimentation with modal interchange and evaluate the impact on the overall mood and expressiveness of your composition.

Example 1 – Scarborough Fair/Canticle by Simon & Garfunkel:

This classic piece incorporates modal interchange, borrowing chords from both major and minor modes, creating a hauntingly beautiful harmonic landscape.

Example 2 – Blackbird by The Beatles:

Blackbird uses modal interchange with borrowed chords, contributing to its intricate and evocative harmonic structure.

Example 3 – Hotel California by Eagles:

The iconic guitar solo section of *Hotel California* features modal interchange, introducing unexpected chords and enriching the harmonic palette.

Experimenting with modal interchange in your guitar composition opens up a world of harmonic possibilities. By judiciously borrowing chords from parallel or related modes, you can inject freshness and intrigue into your music. Remember to maintain a balance between experimentation and musicality, allowing modal interchange to enhance the expressiveness of your guitar compositions.

DIATONIC AND CHROMATIC ELEMENTS

Blend diatonic harmonies (harmonies within the key) with chromatic elements. This combination can create a balance between familiarity and unpredictability.

BLENDING DIATONIC AND CHROMATIC ELEMENTS

Blending diatonic harmonies with chromatic elements in guitar composition is a sophisticated approach that adds color, tension, and expressiveness to your music. By seamlessly integrating both diatonic and chromatic elements, you can create harmonic interest while maintaining a connection to the key.

Understanding Diatonic and Chromatic Harmony:

Diatonic harmony uses the notes of the key, while chromatic harmony introduces notes outside the key. Blending these elements adds complexity and nuance to your composition.

Start with Diatonic Foundation:

Establish a diatonic harmonic foundation based on the key of your composition. Use chords and progressions that naturally fit within the key.

Identify Chromatic Opportunities:

Identify points in your composition where chromaticism can enhance tension, provide resolution, or add unexpected twists. These points often coincide with moments of emotional intensity.

Chromatic Passing Chords:

Introduce chromatic passing chords between diatonic chords. This technique adds smooth transitions and can create a sense of forward motion.

Example:

```

Diatonic: C - G - Am
Chromatic Passing: C - E7 - Am
```

Chromatic Approach Notes:

Use chromatic approach notes to lead into diatonic chords. This can be applied in melody lines or as part of the harmony.

Example:

```

Diatonic: Dm - G7 - C
Chromatic Approach: Dm - G7 - Gdim - C
```

Chromatic Diminished Chords:

Incorporate chromatic diminished chords to create tension before resolving to a diatonic chord.

Example:

```

Diatonic: A - D - E
Chromatic Diminished: A - Adim - D - E
```

Chromatic Passing Tones in Melody:

If you have a melodic line, introduce chromatic passing tones to add color and connect diatonic notes.

Example:

```

Diatonic Melody: C - E - G
Chromatic Passing: C - E - G

```

Chromatic Secondary Dominants:

Include chromatic secondary dominant chords to heighten tension and create strong resolutions.

Example:

```

Diatonic: G - C - Am
Chromatic Secondary Dominant: G - D7 - Am

```

Chromatic Pedal Tones:

Use chromatic pedal tones in the bass to create a sense of continuity while harmonies change above.

Example:

```

Diatonic: C - G - Am
Chromatic Pedal: C - G/B - Am

```

Chromatic Voice Leading:

Employ chromatic voice leading between diatonic chords, creating smooth transitions and enhancing the overall cohesion of your composition.

Example:
```

Diatonic: Em - Am - D

Chromatic Voice Leading: Em - E7 - Adim - Am - D
```


Chromatic Altered Dominant Chords:

Introduce chromatic altered dominant chords to add tension and excitement, leading to diatonic resolutions.
Example:
```

Diatonic: G - C - D

Chromatic Altered Dominant: G75 - C - D
```


Chromatic Passing Bass Lines:

Experiment with chromatic passing bass lines that connect diatonic chords, creating movement and interest.
Example:
```

Diatonic: F - Bb - C

Chromatic Passing Bass: F - F - Bb - C
```


Chromatic Sequences:

Create chromatic sequences within diatonic progressions to build tension and surprise.

Example:
```

Diatonic: Dm - G - C
Chromatic Sequence: Dm - Gdim - G - C
```

Chromatic Melodic Embellishments:
Enhance diatonic melodies with chromatic embellishments. These can include slides, bends, or additional chromatic notes.
Example:
```

Diatonic Melody: A - B - C
Chromatic Embellishments: A - Bb - B - C
```

Record and Refine:
Record your composition to hear how diatonic and chromatic elements interact. Refine the balance to achieve the desired expressive impact.

Example 1 – All the Things You Are by Jerome Kern:
This jazz standard masterfully blends diatonic and chromatic elements, creating a rich harmonic tapestry.

Example 2 – Scarborough Fair/Canticle by Simon & Garfunkel:
The use of chromatic elements in this piece adds a touch of melancholy, blending seamlessly with the diatonic folk–style harmonies.

Example 3 – Purple Haze by Jimi Hendrix:

Jimi Hendrix's iconic riff in *Purple Haze* combines diatonic and chromatic elements, creating a groundbreaking harmonic language.

Blending diatonic harmonies with chromatic elements in your guitar composition opens up a realm of creative possibilities. The key is to use chromaticism judiciously, enhancing the emotional impact of your music while maintaining a connection to the diatonic foundation. Experiment with these techniques, and let the interplay between diatonic and chromatic elements elevate the expressiveness of your guitar compositions.

HARMONIC PEDALS

Introduce harmonic pedals, where a particular harmony is sustained while the underlying chords change. This technique can create a sense of stability or tension.

USING HARMONIC PEDALS

Harmonic pedals, often referred to as pedal points or drone notes, are static, sustained tones that persist throughout chord changes or progressions. Integrating harmonic pedals into your guitar composition can create a sense of stability, tension, or color, providing a unique sonic texture.

Understanding Harmonic Pedals:

Harmonic pedals involve sustaining a single pitch or a set of pitches while harmonies around them change. This creates a point of reference amidst harmonic movement.

Choose a Harmonic Pedal Tone:

Select a note or a set of notes that resonate with the overall mood of your composition. Common choices include the tonic, dominant, or a note from an extended chord.

Harmonic Pedal on the Root:

Sustain the tonic note throughout chord changes, creating a grounded and stable foundation.

Example:
```

Chord Progression: C - Am - F - G
Harmonic Pedal: C sustained throughout
```


Harmonic Pedal on the Dominant:
Use the dominant note as a pedal to introduce tension, anticipating resolutions.
Example:
```

Chord Progression: G - Em - C - D
Harmonic Pedal: G sustained throughout
```


Harmonic Pedal on a Chord Extension:
Choose a pedal tone from an extended chord (e.g., 7th, 9th) to add color and complexity.
Example:
```

Chord Progression: Dm7 - G7 - Cmaj7
Harmonic Pedal: G sustained throughout (7th of Dm7)
```


Shifting Harmonic Pedals:
Experiment with shifting the harmonic pedal tone along with chord changes to create dynamic movement.

Example:
```

Chord Progression: C - G/B - Am - G
Shifting Pedal: C to G/B to A sustained
```

Pedal on Open Strings:

Utilize open strings as harmonic pedals, providing a rich and resonant quality to your composition.

Example:
```

Chord Progression: E - A - B
Open String Pedal: E string sustained throughout
```

Incorporate Pedals in Fingerstyle Patterns:

Integrate harmonic pedals into fingerstyle patterns, sustaining notes within the picking or plucking sequence.

Example:
```

Fingerstyle Pattern: C - G - Am - F
Harmonic Pedal: G sustained during entire pattern
```

Pedals in Arpeggiated Sequences:

Include harmonic pedals within arpeggiated sequences, emphasizing sustained tones in the midst of arpeggios.

Example:
```

Arpeggio Sequence: Dm - G - C
Harmonic Pedal: D sustained throughout
```

Harmonic Pedal as a Point of Rest:

Use a harmonic pedal as a point of rest between chord changes, offering moments of tranquility.

Example:
```

Chord Progression: Em - C - G - D
Harmonic Pedal: G sustained during transitions
```

Contrast Pedals with Dynamic Chords:

Introduce harmonic pedals during quieter, more reflective sections, contrasting with dynamic chord progressions.

Example:
```

Dynamic Section: G - D - Em - C
Harmonic Pedal Section: Em sustained throughout
```

Layer Harmonic Pedals for Texture:

Experiment with layering multiple harmonic pedals, creating intricate textures and harmonies.

Example:
```

Chord Progression: D - A - G
Harmonic Pedals: D and G sustained simultaneously
```

Pedal in Modal Context:
Utilize harmonic pedals to emphasize modal characteristics, especially in compositions with modal tonalities.
Example:
```

Modal Section: Dm - G - Am
Harmonic Pedal: D sustained throughout (D Dorian)
```

Blend Pedals with Melodic Lines:
Integrate harmonic pedals into melodic lines, creating a seamless blend of sustained tones and moving phrases.
Example:
```

Melody: C - E - G
Harmonic Pedal: E sustained throughout
```

Record and Adjust:

Record your composition with harmonic pedals and actively listen to ensure the desired balance and impact. Make adjustments as needed.

Example 1 – Babe I'm Gonna Leave You by Led Zeppelin:

This classic rock song features harmonic pedals on open strings, creating a haunting and atmospheric quality.

Example 2 – Dust in the Wind by Kansas:

The arpeggiated sections of this song incorporate sustained harmonic pedals, contributing to its ethereal and contemplative atmosphere.

Example 3 – Blackbird by The Beatles:

Blackbird incorporates harmonic pedals within its fingerstyle pattern, enhancing the overall expressiveness of the composition.

Incorporating harmonic pedals into your guitar composition can add depth, tension, and a unique sonic character. Whether as points of stability, tension, or color, these sustained tones provide a foundation for the evolving harmonies around them. Experiment with different pedal tones and contexts to discover the rich possibilities they bring to your musical creations.

UNISON AND OCTAVES

Consider incorporating moments of unison or octaves between the melody and harmonies. These intervals can add emphasis and create impactful sonic moments.

USING UNISON AND OCTAVES

Incorporating moments of unison or octaves between the melody and harmonies in guitar composition can create a powerful and unified sound. This technique adds richness and emphasis to specific musical passages, enhancing the overall impact of your composition.

Choosing Strategic Moments:

Select specific moments within your composition where unison or octaves can highlight key phrases, climactic sections, or points of emotional intensity.

Enhancing Melodic Emphasis:

Use unison or octaves to emphasize important melodic lines. This technique can draw attention to a particular motif or theme, making it stand out within the overall arrangement.

Amplifying Climactic Sections:

Reserve unison or octave passages for climactic sections of your composition. This adds a sense of intensity and energy, elevating the emotional impact.

Balancing Dynamics:

Consider the dynamic level when incorporating unison or octaves. This technique is particularly effective when used during louder, more dynamic sections to create a bold and unified sound.

Building Transitions:

Use unison or octaves as transitional elements between different sections. This helps maintain a cohesive flow while adding a sense of anticipation.

Utilizing Open Strings:

Take advantage of open strings to enhance the resonance and sustain of unison or octave passages. This can contribute to a fuller and more resonant sound.

Combining with Harmonies:

Experiment with combining unison or octaves with harmonies. This creates a layered and textured effect, adding depth to the overall sound.

Applying Articulation Techniques:

Experiment with different articulation techniques such as legato, staccato, or slides when playing unison or octave passages. These techniques can add nuance and character to the sound.

Maintaining Clarity:

Ensure that unison or octave passages maintain clarity in the context of the entire arrangement. Be mindful of the harmonic context to prevent potential clashes.

Examples:

Example 1 - Climactic Emphasis:
```

Melody: | CG| AmF|
Harmony: | CG| AmF|
```

In this example, unison or octave passages are used during the climactic progression, emphasizing the chord changes.

Example 2 - Transitional Element:
```

Melody: | GD| EmC|
Harmony: | GD| EmC|
```

Unison or octaves are utilized as a transitional element between different chord progressions, smoothing the transition.

Example 3 - Layered Effect:
```

Melody: | AmG| FE|
Harmony: | AmG| FE|
Bass:| A G| FE|
```

Unison or octave passages are combined with harmonies and a bass line, creating a layered and textured effect.

Example 4 – Dynamic Climax:
```

Melody: | DG| AD|
Harmony: | DG| AD|
```

Unison or octaves are reserved for a dynamic climax, amplifying the impact of the chord progression.

Example 5 – Articulation Variation:
```

Melody: | CE| DG|
Harmony: | CE| DG|
```

Unison passages are played with varied articulation, utilizing slides or legato to add expressiveness.

Recording and Evaluating:

Record your composition to evaluate how unison or octave passages contribute to the overall sound. Adjust the balance and placement of these moments as needed.

Incorporating moments of unison or octaves between the melody and harmonies in guitar composition requires thoughtful consideration of the musical context and desired emotional impact. Discover how these techniques can enhance the unity and intensity of your musical creations.

ITERATE AND REFINE

As with any compositional element, be prepared to iterate and refine your harmonies. Continuously assess how they contribute to the overall mood and expression of your composition.

EXPLORE ITERATION AND REFINEMENT

Iterating and refining your harmonies is a crucial aspect of the composition process, allowing you to polish and enhance the musical depth of your piece.

Initial Sketch:

Begin with a basic harmonic structure for your composition. This could be a chord progression that captures the essence of your musical idea.

Experiment with Variations:

Introduce variations to your initial harmonic sketch. Try different chord voicings, inversions, or substitutions to explore alternative harmonic possibilities.

Evaluate Emotional Impact:

Assess the emotional impact of each harmonic variation. Consider whether the changes align with the mood and atmosphere you intend to convey in your composition.

Voice Leading:

Pay attention to the smoothness of voice leading between chords. Refine transitions to ensure that individual voices move naturally from one chord to the next.

Explore Extended Chords:

Experiment with extended chords (sevenths, ninths, elevenths) to add complexity and color to your harmonies. See how these extensions contribute to the overall harmonic palette.

Evaluate Balance Across Sections:

Ensure a balanced harmonic progression across different sections of your composition. Evaluate how well the harmonies flow from one section to another.

Add Subtle Modulations:

Introduce subtle modulations to different keys or tonal centers. This can create a sense of journey and development in your composition.

Include Harmonic Sequences:

Implement harmonic sequences where a specific pattern of chords repeats or evolves. This technique can create structure and coherence in your harmonies.

Record and Listen:

Record your playing and actively listen to the recorded harmonies. This provides an objective perspective and helps identify areas for improvement.

Collaborate with Others:

Collaborate with other musicians to get fresh insights into your harmonies. Different perspectives can lead to valuable refinements.

Evaluate Rhythmic Aspects:

Consider how rhythmic elements interact with your harmonies. Experiment with syncopation or changes in harmonic rhythm to add rhythmic interest.

Refine Dynamic Changes:

Adjust dynamic changes within your harmonies. Determine where crescendos or diminuendos can enhance the overall expressive quality of your composition.

Example 1 – Basic Progression:
```

Original: | CG| AmF|
```

Begin with a simple progression. Iterate by experimenting with different voicings, perhaps trying an inversion of the Am chord.

Example 2 – Extended Chords:
```

Original: | DmG| CE7|
```

Extend chords to add complexity:
```

Refined: | Dm7G9| Cmaj7E79|
```

Example 3 – Subtle Modulation:
```

Original: | EmAm| DG|
```

```
Introduce a subtle modulation:
```

```
Refined: | EmAm| BmE|
```


Example 4 – Harmonic Sequence:
```

```
Original: | CF| GC|
```

```
Create a harmonic sequence:
```

```
Refined: | CF| GC| AmDm| GC|
```


Example 5 – Collaborative Refinement:
Collaborate with another musician, refining harmonies for a shared vision. Experiment with their suggestions to find harmonies that resonate with both of you.

Iterative Recording:

Record multiple iterations of your composition, incorporating refinements at each step. Listen to the recordings to track your progress and identify areas that still need attention.

Evaluate Harmony with Melody:

Ensure harmony aligns well with the melody. Refine harmonies to support and enhance the melodic lines, creating a cohesive musical narrative.
```

Final Iteration:

After several rounds of iteration and refinement, arrive at a harmonically rich version that best encapsulates your musical vision.

Seek Feedback:

Share your refined harmonies with others and gather constructive feedback. This external input can offer valuable perspectives and further refine your composition.

Document Your Process:

Keep a record of your iterative process, including changes made and the reasoning behind them. This documentation serves as a reference for future compositions.

Iterating and refining harmonies is an ongoing and rewarding process. Embrace experimentation, stay open to new ideas, and use each iteration to bring your composition closer to its full potential.

Harmonizing a melody on the guitar offers a vast canvas for creative exploration. Trust your musical intuition, be open to experimentation, and enjoy the process of discovering harmonies that bring depth and beauty to your guitar composition.

IN CLOSING

As we enter the closing chapter of this book, it's essential to reflect on the incredible journey we've undertaken together. From the foundational principles of melody development to the intricate complexities of harmony construction, you've delved deep into the heart of guitar composition. Through dedication, exploration, and a relentless pursuit of excellence, you've expanded your musical horizons and honed your craft to new heights.

Yet, this journey is far from over. As you close this book and return to your guitar, remember that mastery is a lifelong pursuit. Every note you play, every chord you strum, is an opportunity for growth and expression. Embrace each moment with passion and purpose, and let the melodies and harmonies flow freely from your fingertips.

As you continue to compose and create, don't be afraid to push the boundaries of convention. Experiment with new techniques, explore uncharted musical territories, and let your creativity run wild. It is through bold experimentation and fearless innovation that true artistic greatness is achieved.

And remember, the journey of a guitarist is not a solitary one. Seek inspiration from fellow musicians, collaborate with others, and immerse yourself in the rich tapestry of musical collaboration. By sharing your talents and insights with others, you enrich not only your own musical journey but the collective experience of all who listen.

Above all, never lose sight of the joy and passion that brought you to the guitar in the first place. Whether you're performing on stage, composing in the studio, or simply strumming in the comfort of your own home, let the music be your guide and your inspiration. For in the end, it is the connection between artist and instrument, between player and listener, that truly makes music come alive.

So go forth, dear guitarist, and continue to weave your musical magic. With each new composition, each new performance, you add to the rich tapestry of human expression. Let your melodies soar, your harmonies resound, and your love for the guitar shine bright for all the world to see.

THANK YOU for purchasing *Strings Of Brilliance: Mastering Melody And Harmony Development For Guitar Composition* by University Scholastic Press. If you liked this book, please consider spreading your good word!

University Scholastic Press is an internationally renowned publisher and press, writing and producing textbooks, study guides, quote books, workbooks, cookbooks, journals, planners and creative nonfiction novels.

With offices in New York, London and Rome, University Scholastic Press is the trusted leader in producing and writing classic, bestselling books with an original, polished spin.

Other Musician's Series Books
By University Scholastic Press:

A Guitarist's Grimoire: Unlocking the Secrets of Creating A Musical Diary To Master Guitar Composition

Storytelling With Sound: Fundamentals of Creative Guitar Composition

Musical Architecture Secrets: Structure Planning For Guitar Composition

Strings Of Brilliance: Mastering Melody and Harmony Development For Guitar Composition

Rhythm Mastery for Guitarists: Unlocking Tempo and Timing Techniques For Guitar Composition

Index